Steidl

COTTON ROSE

JITKA HANZLOVÁ

COTTON ROSE

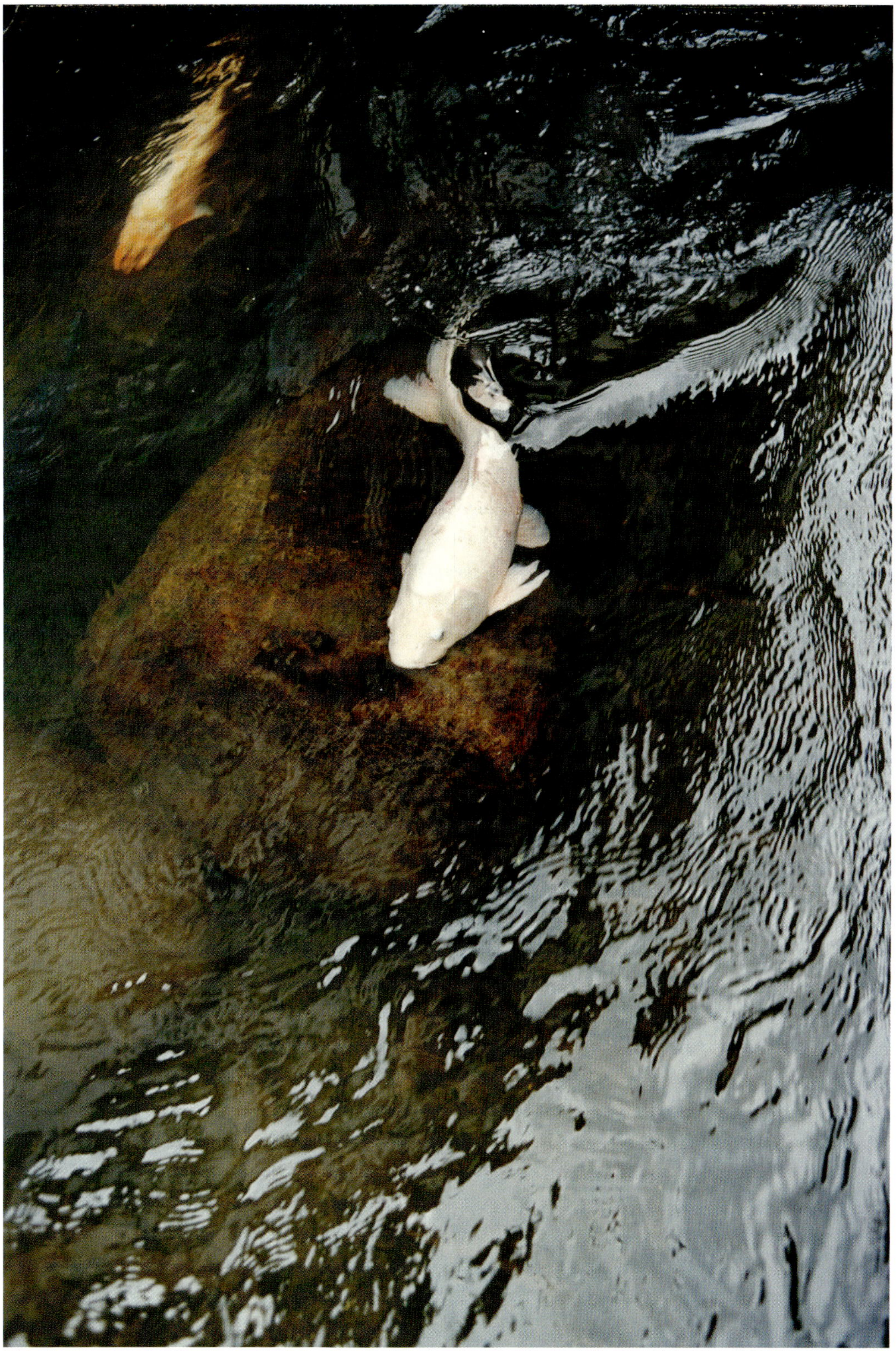

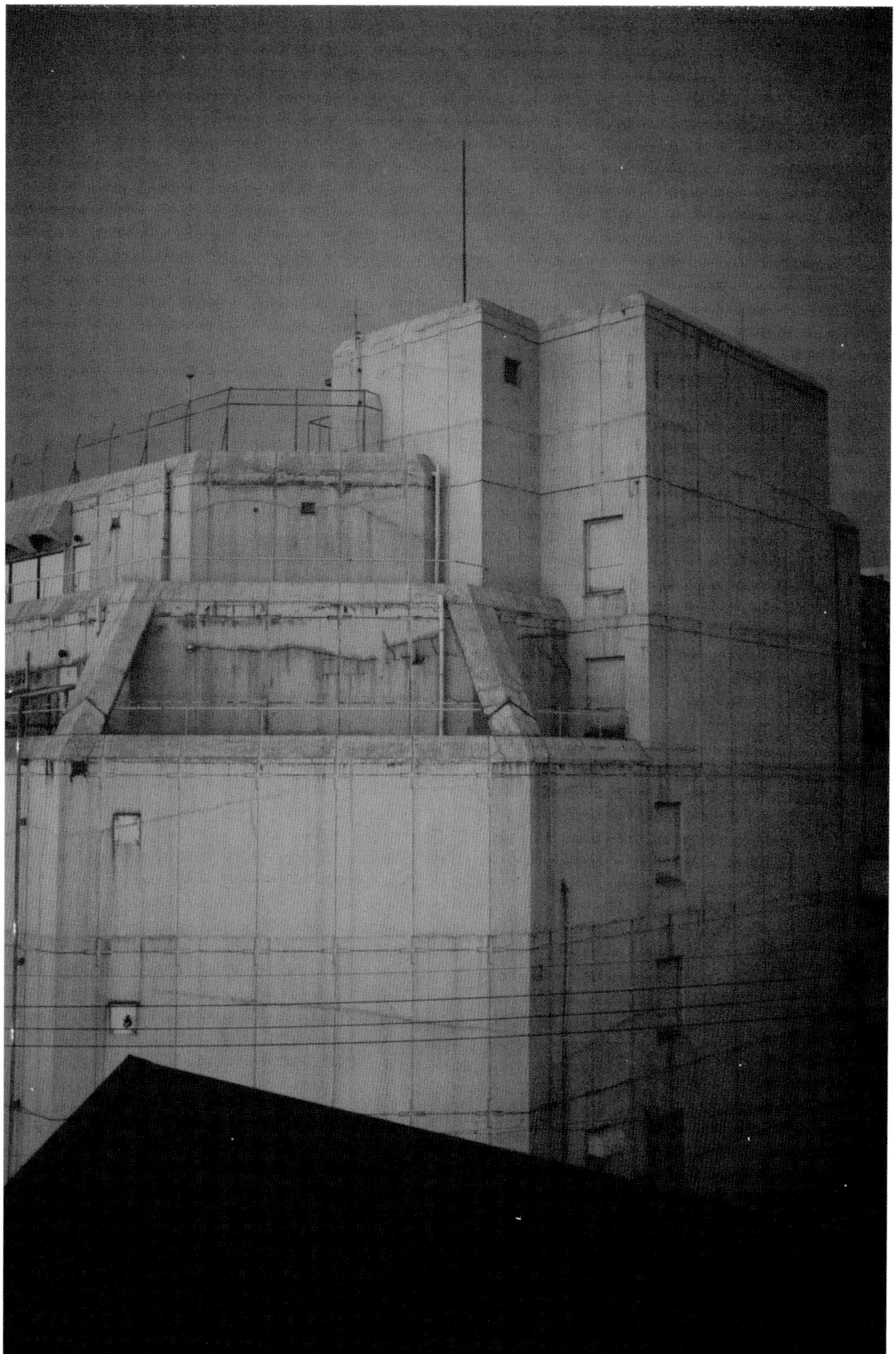

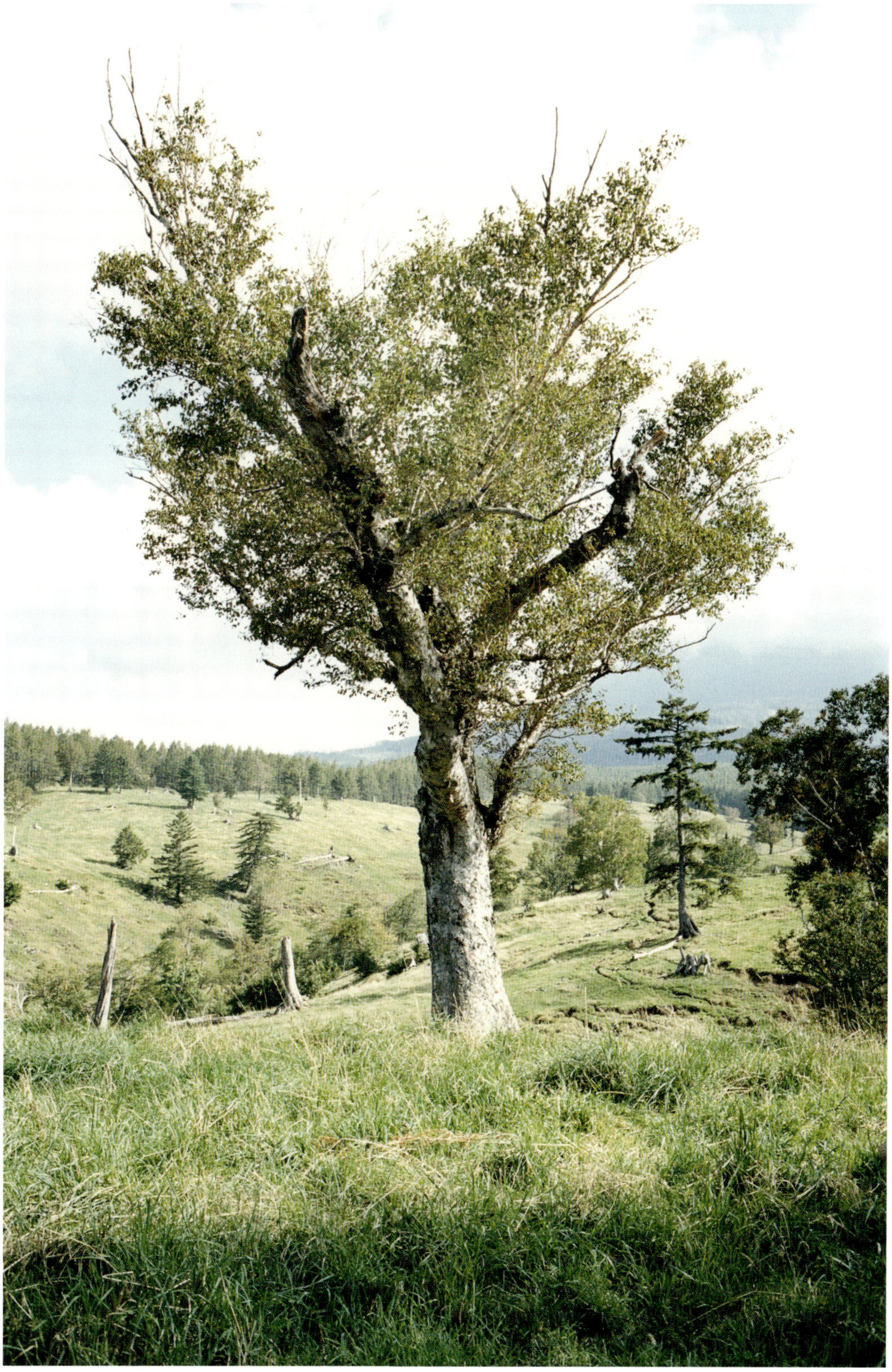

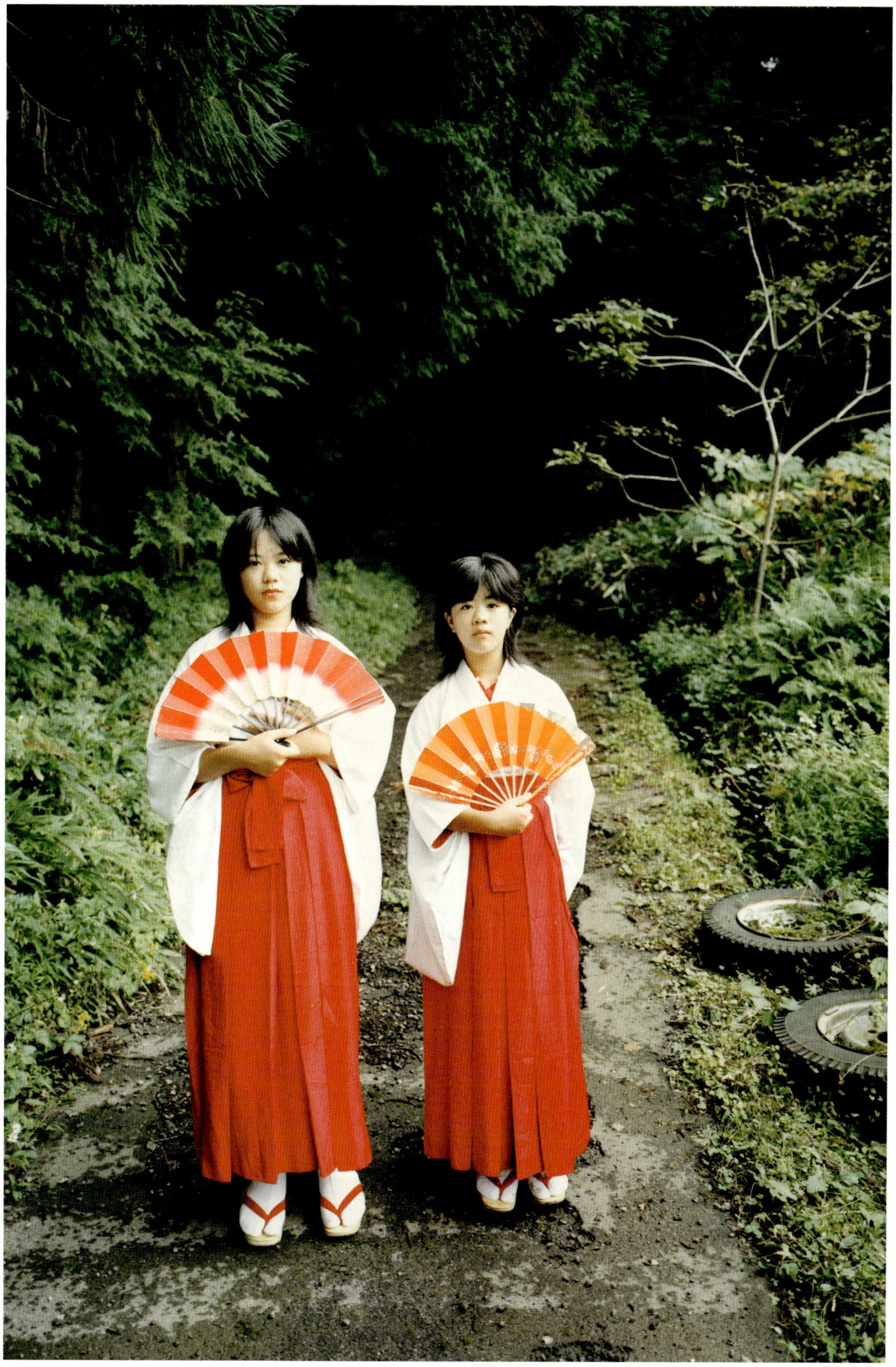

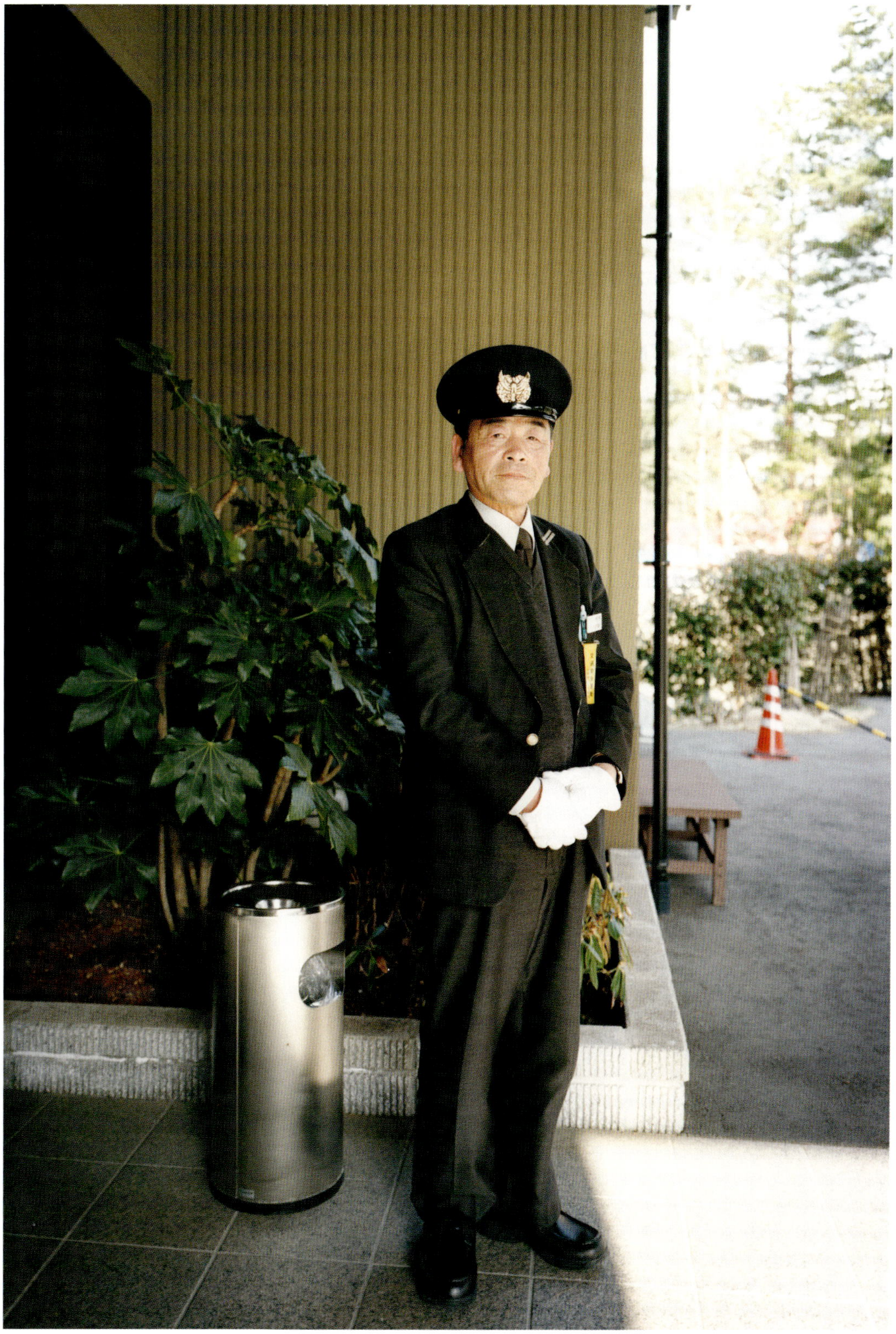

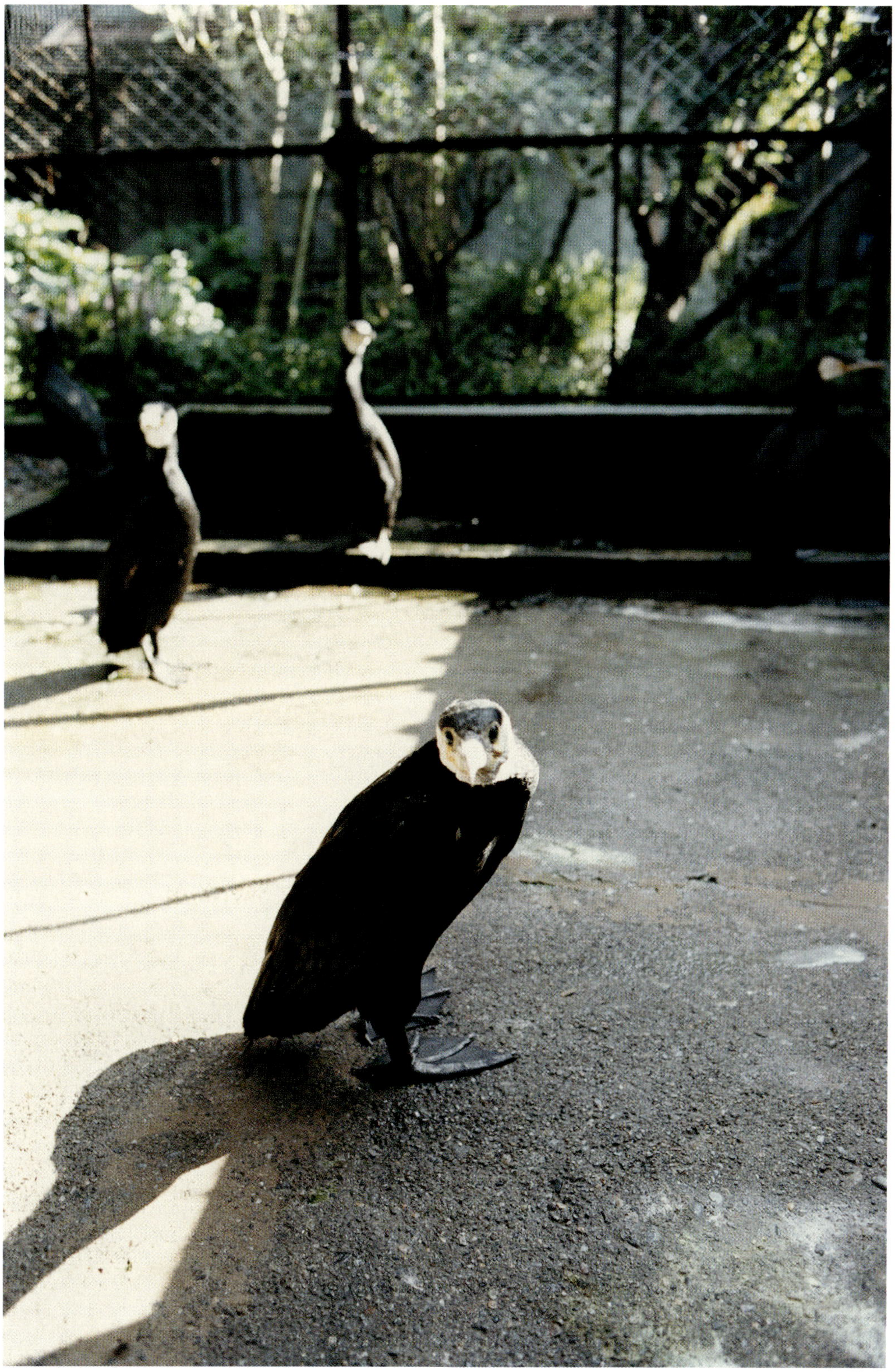

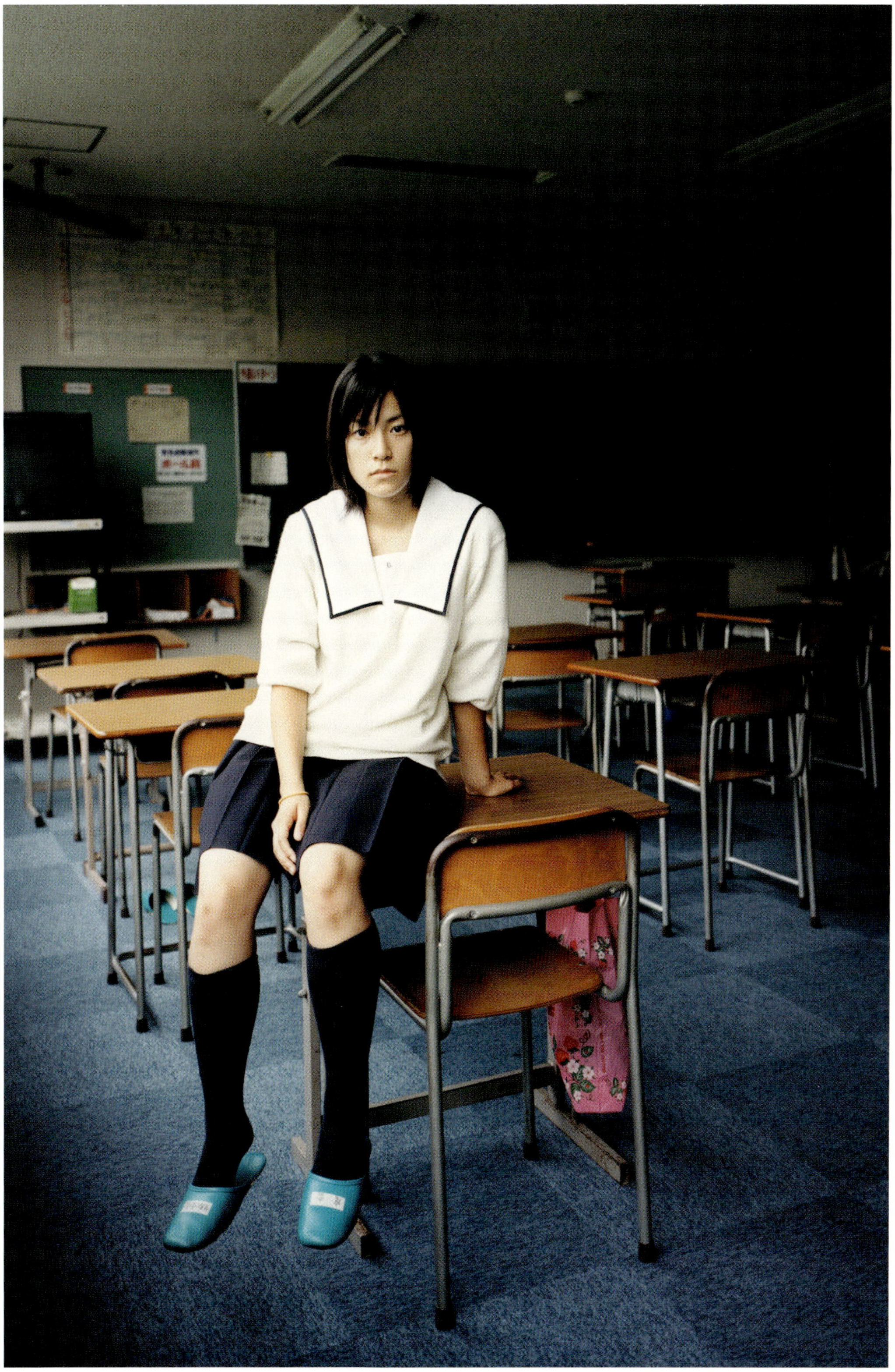

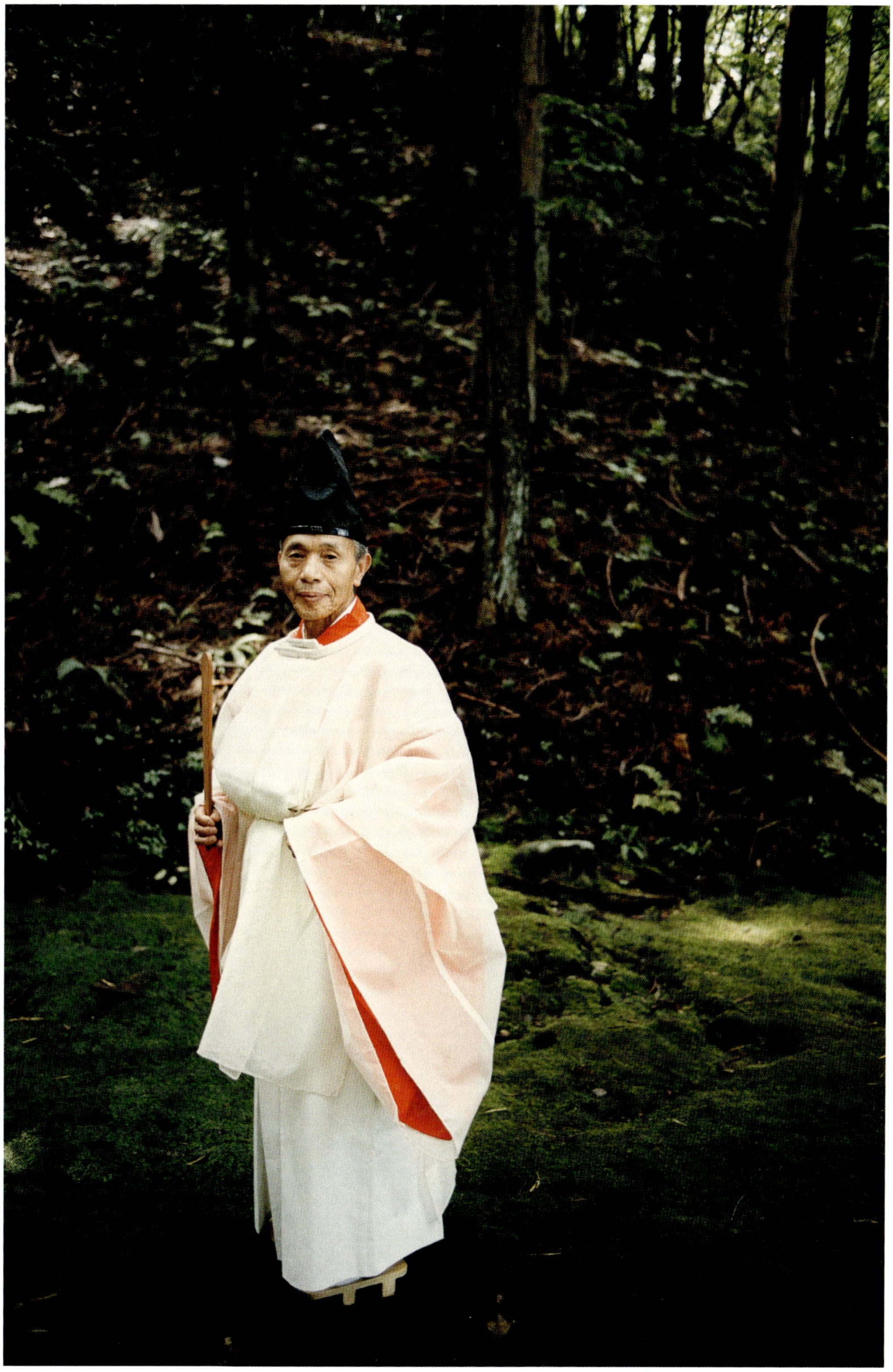

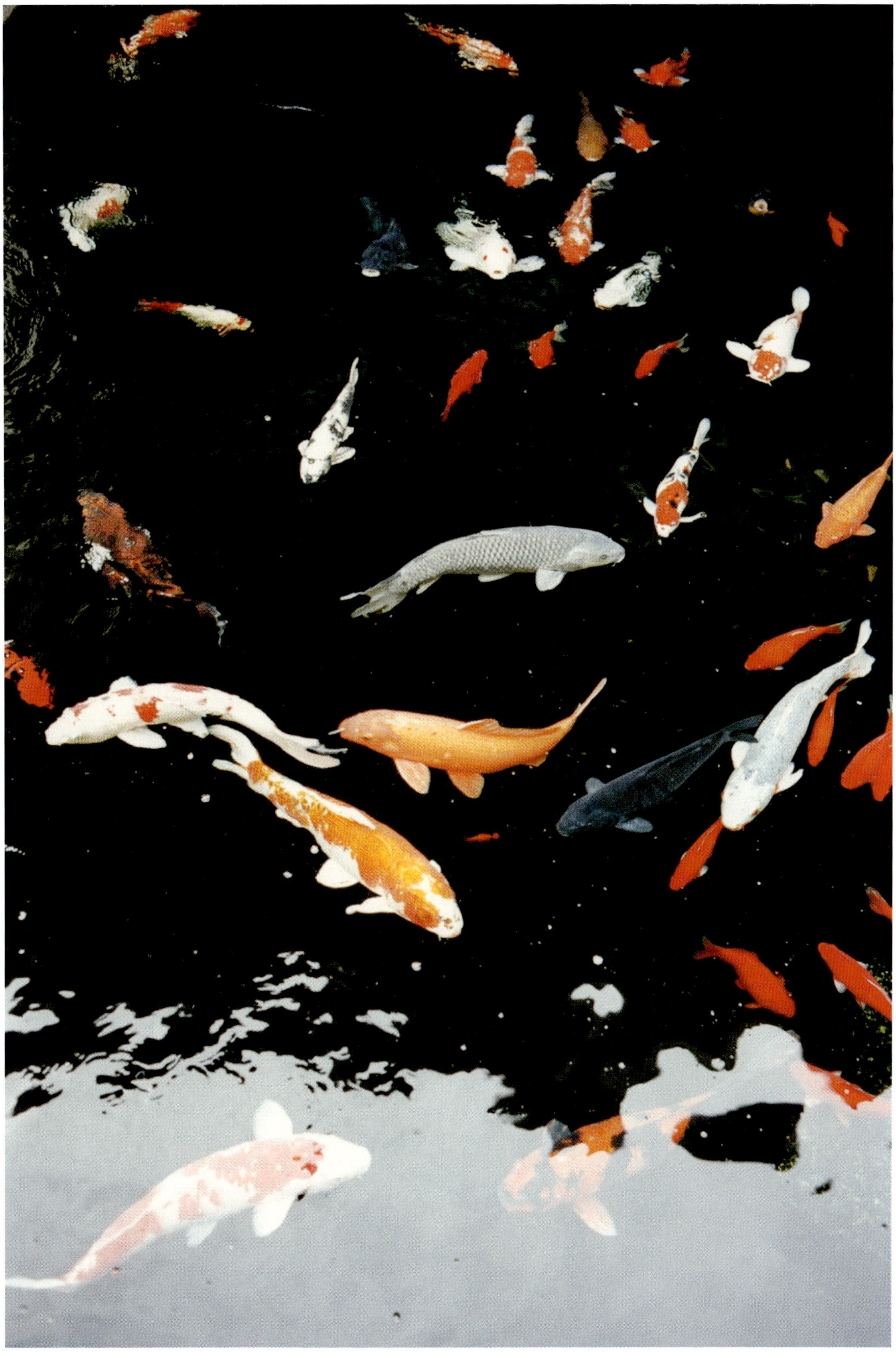

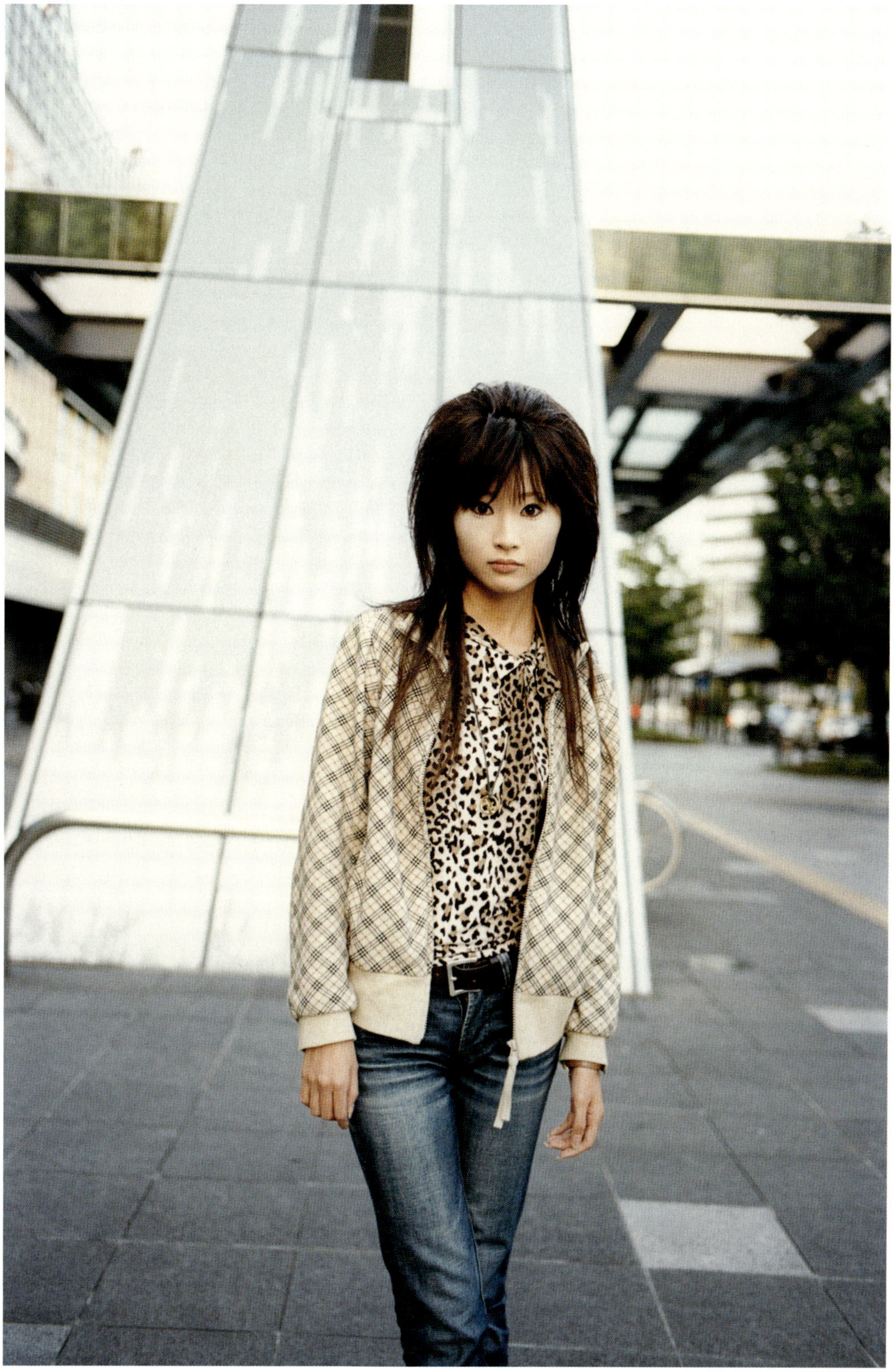

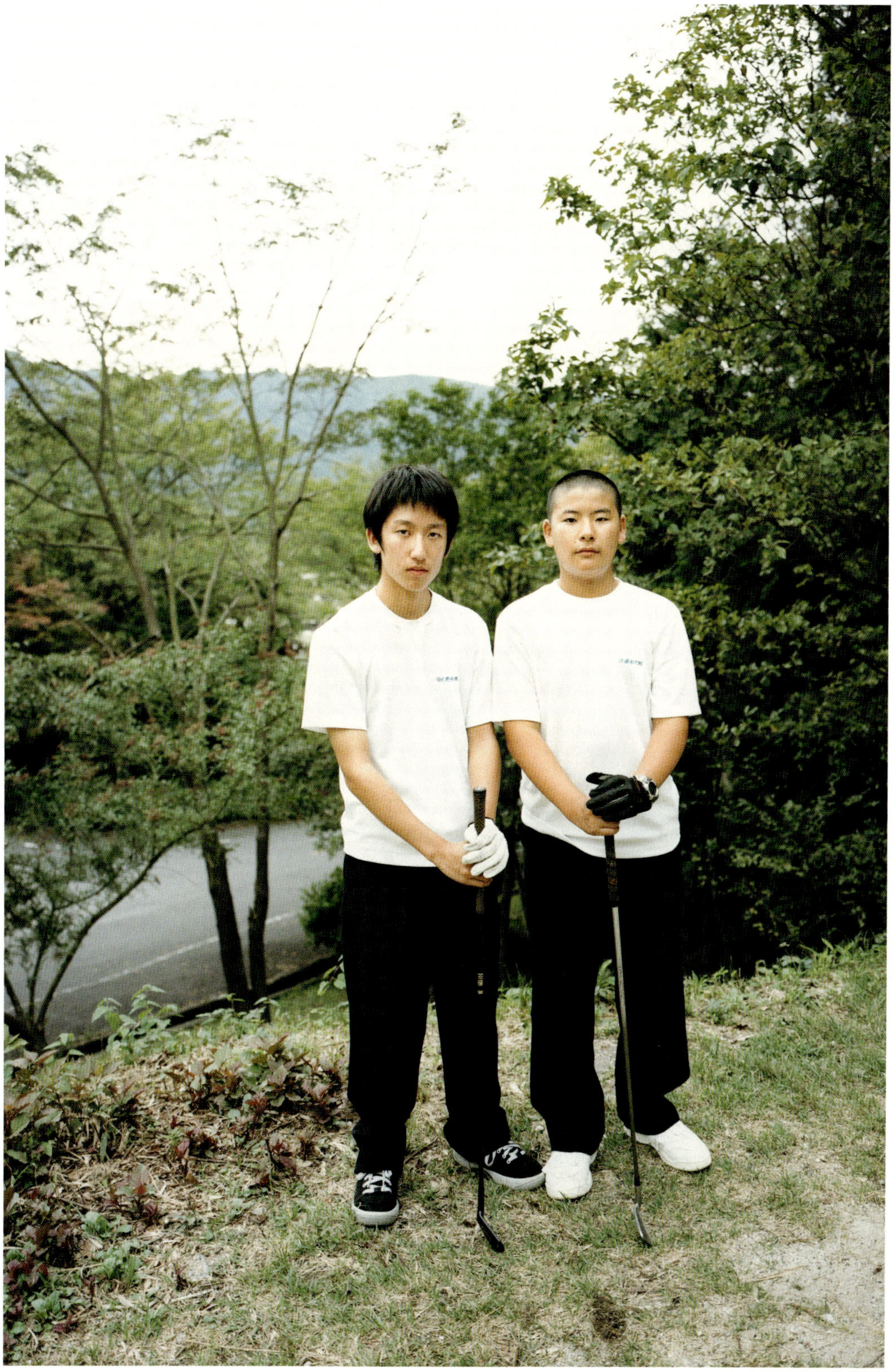

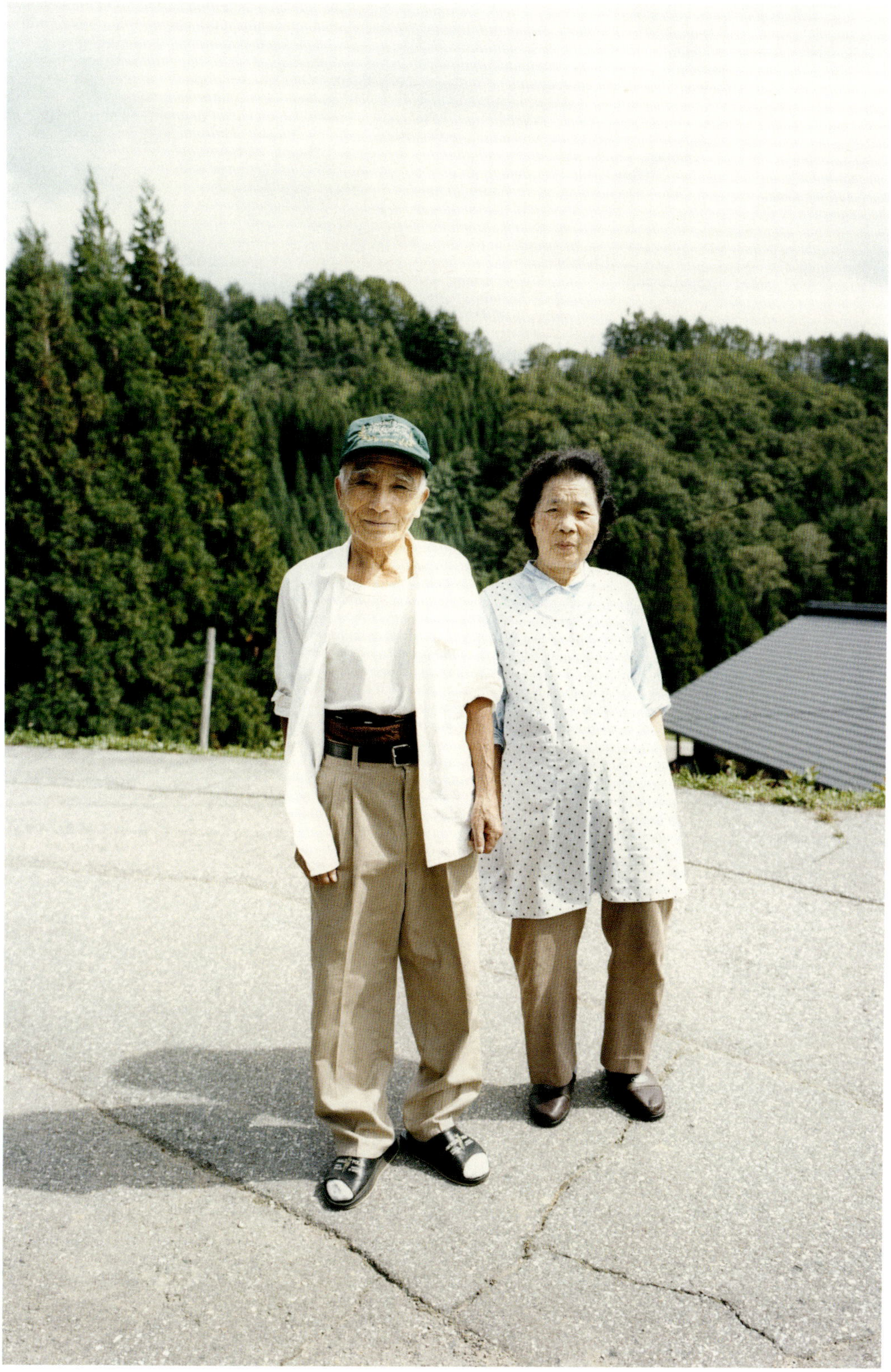

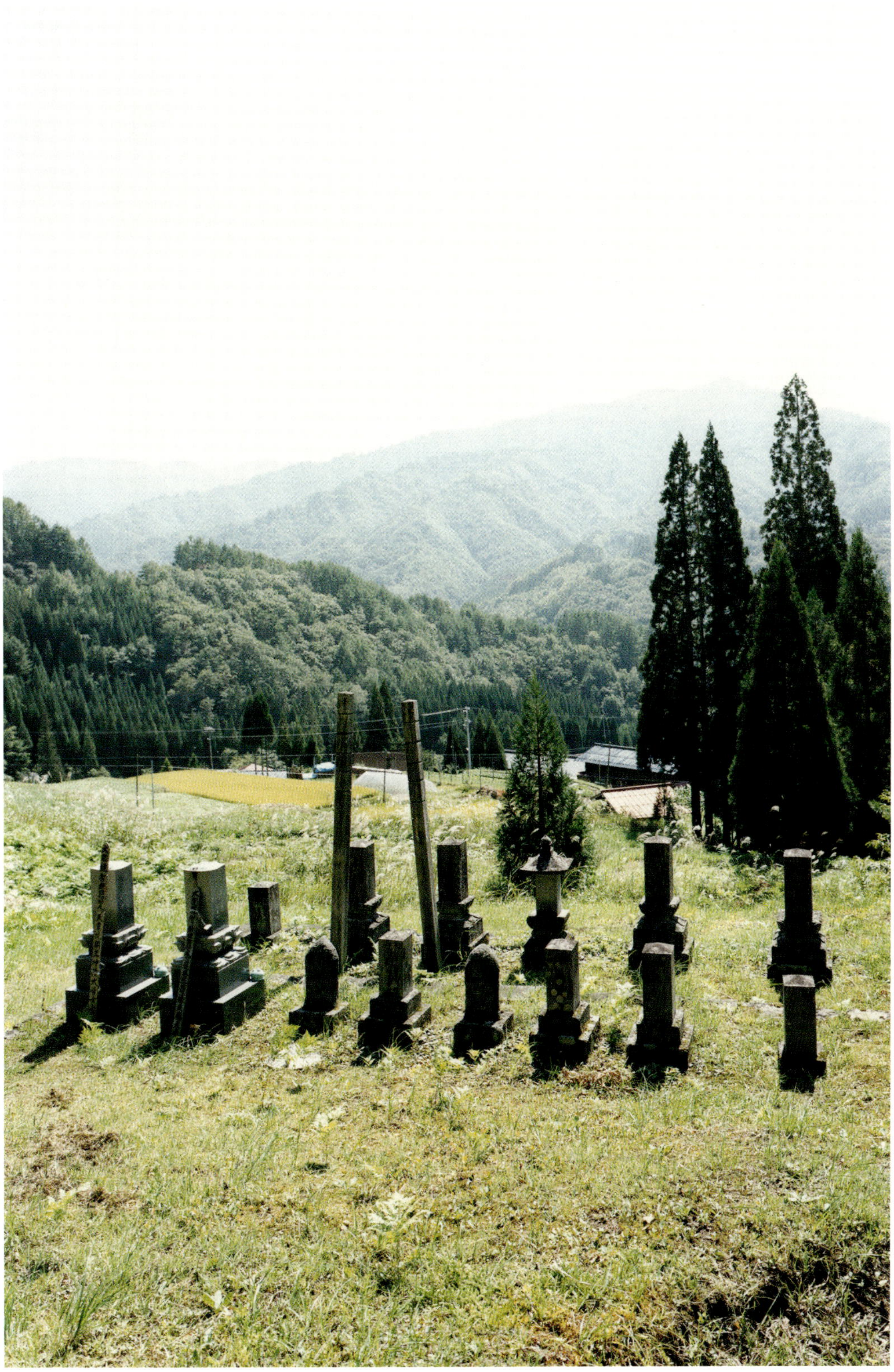

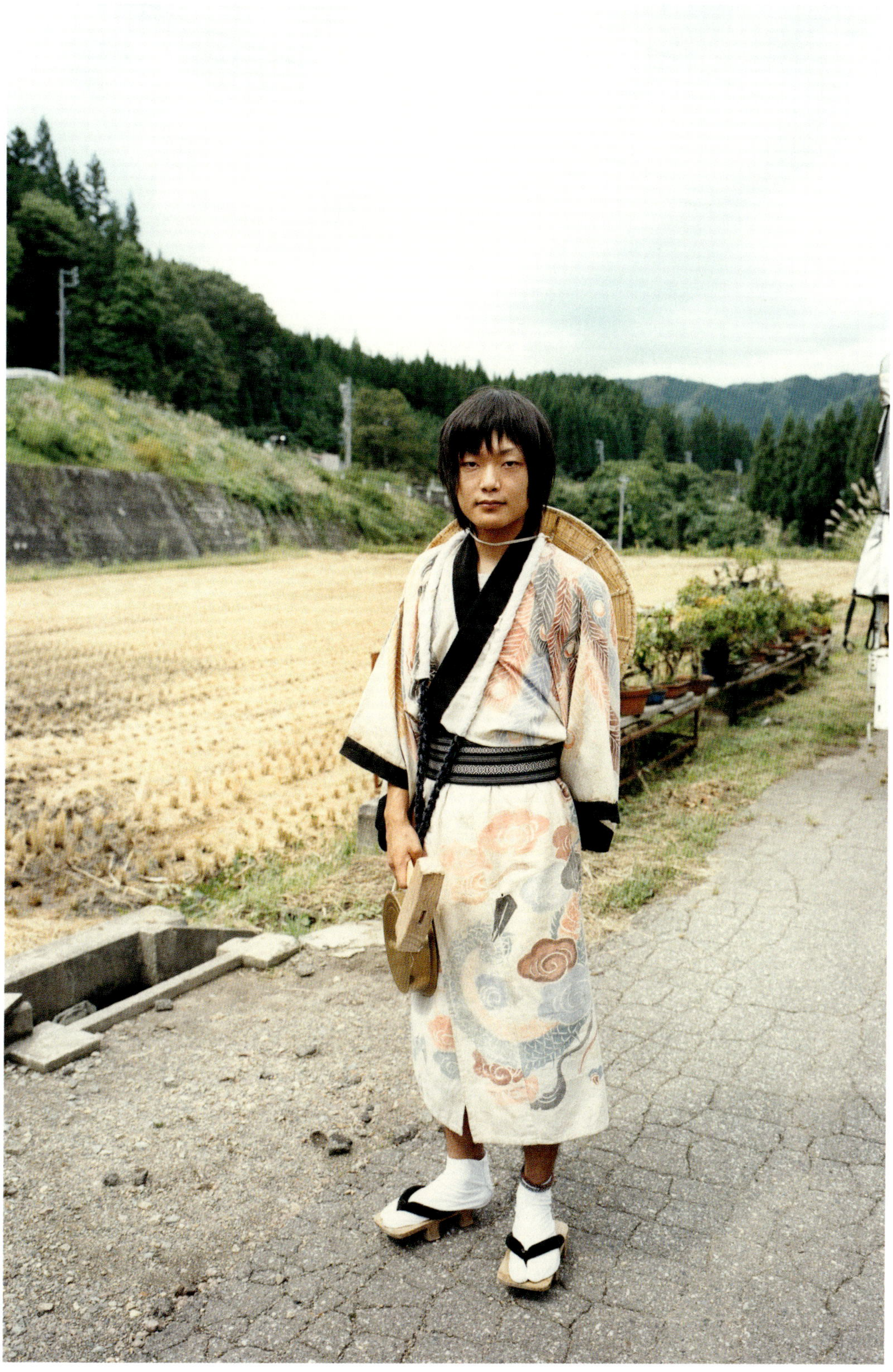

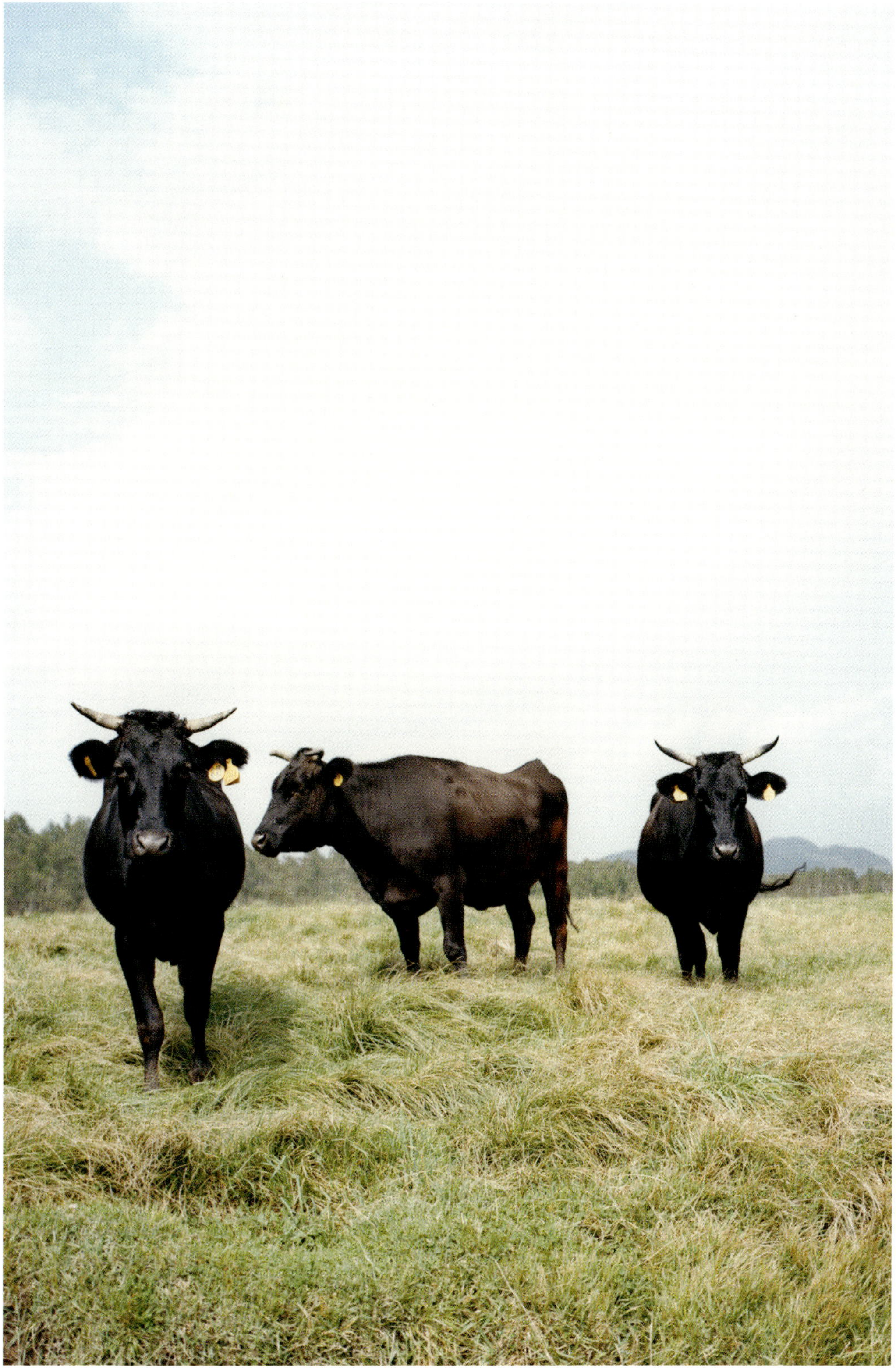

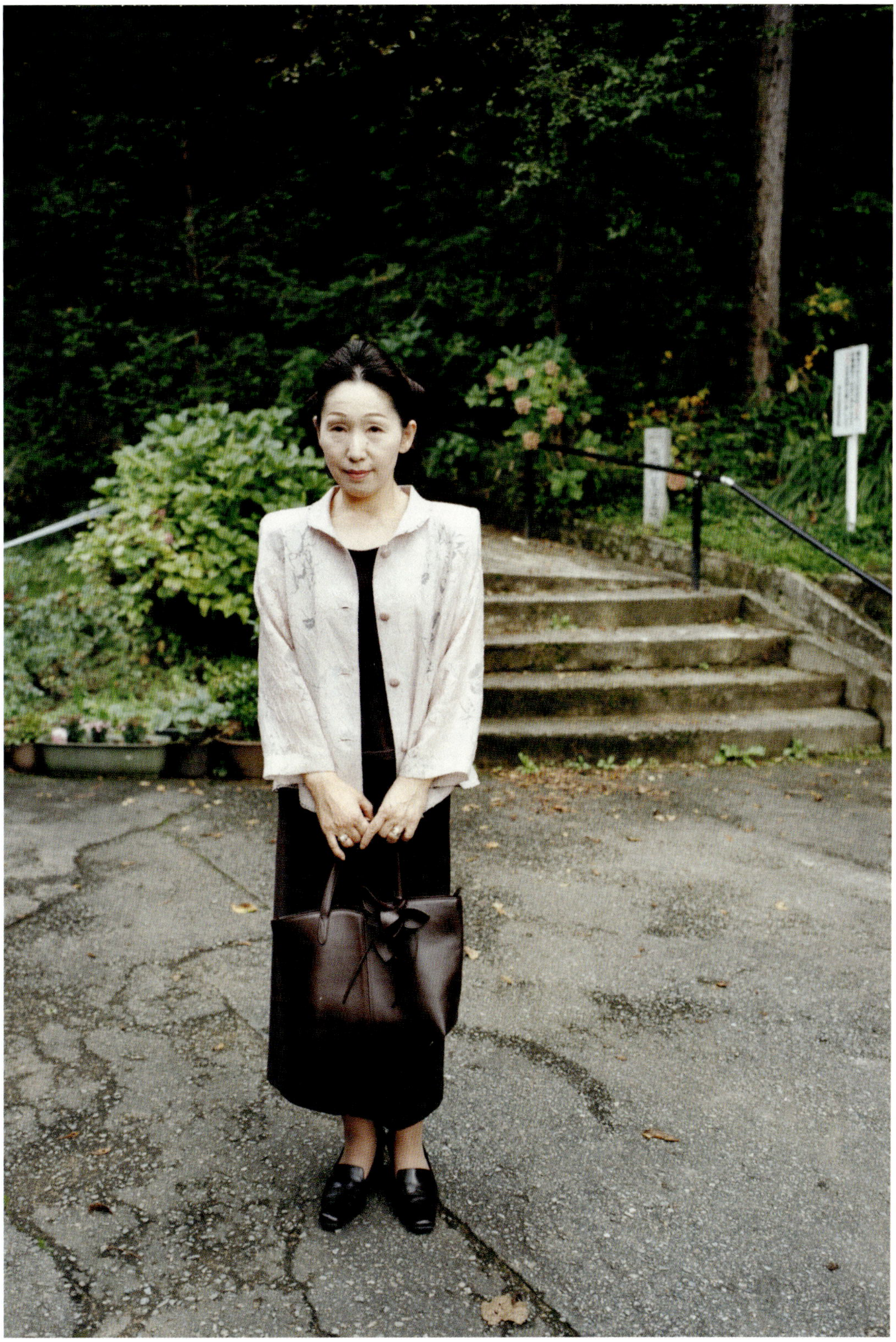

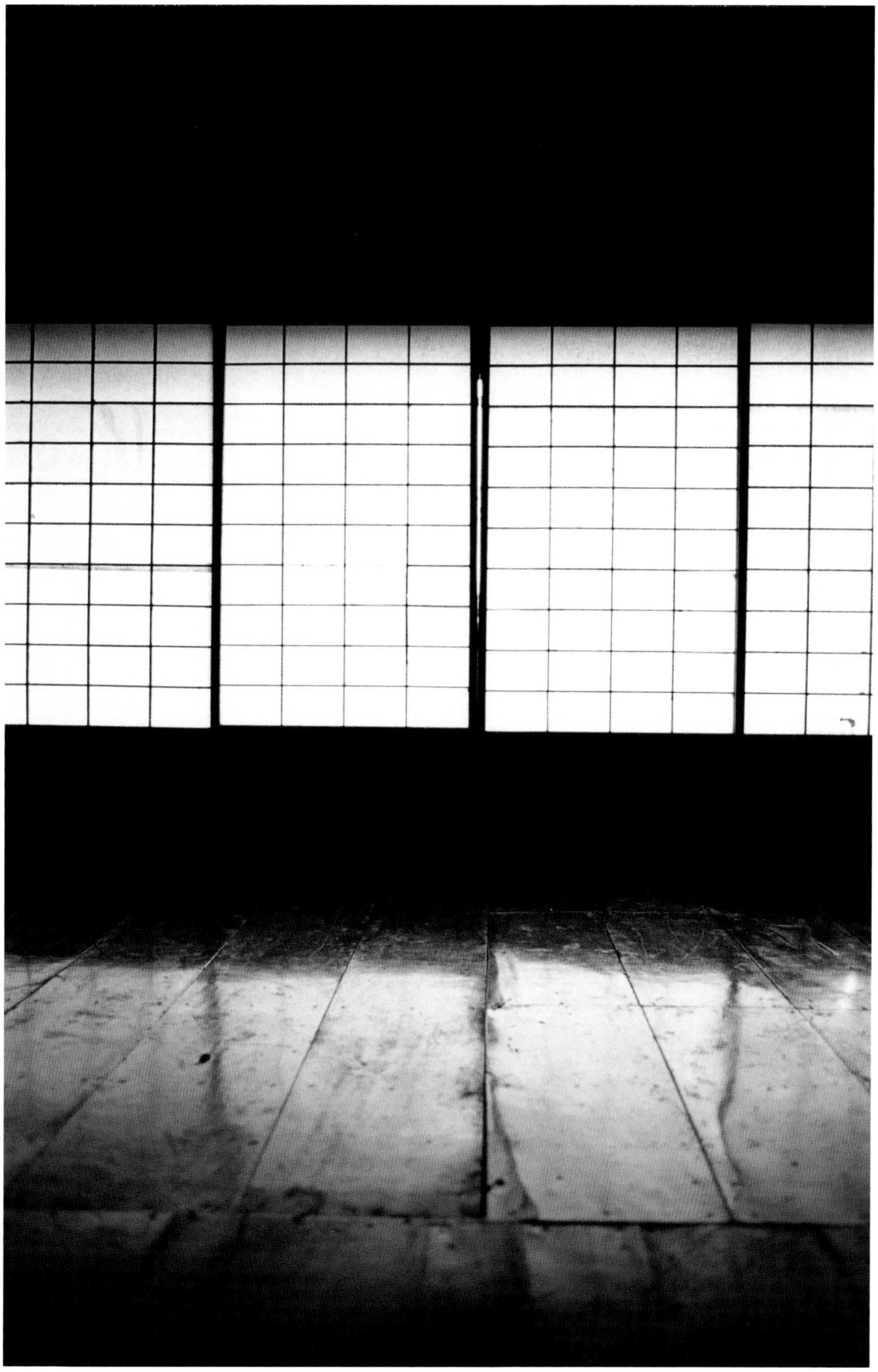

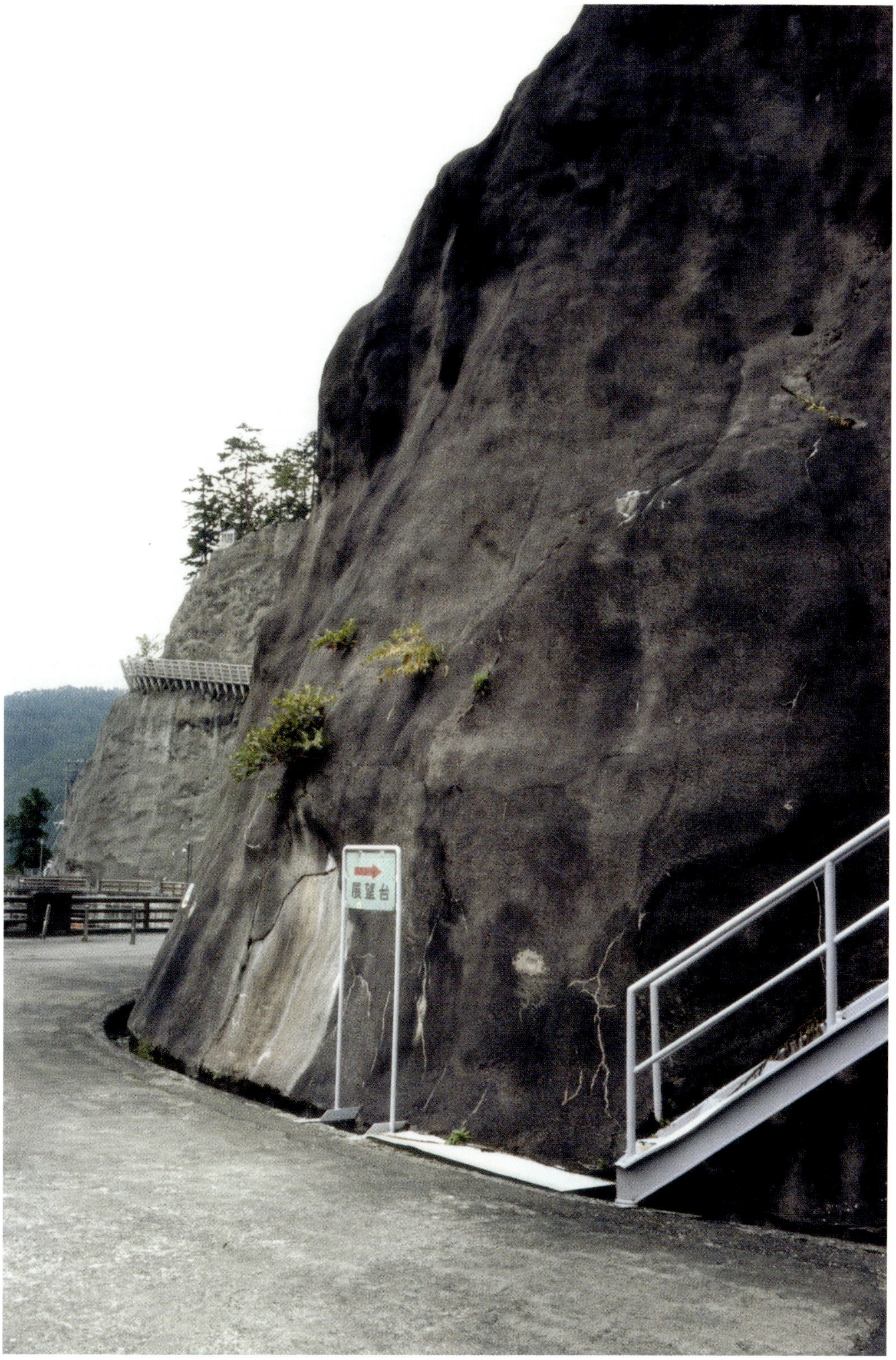
展望台

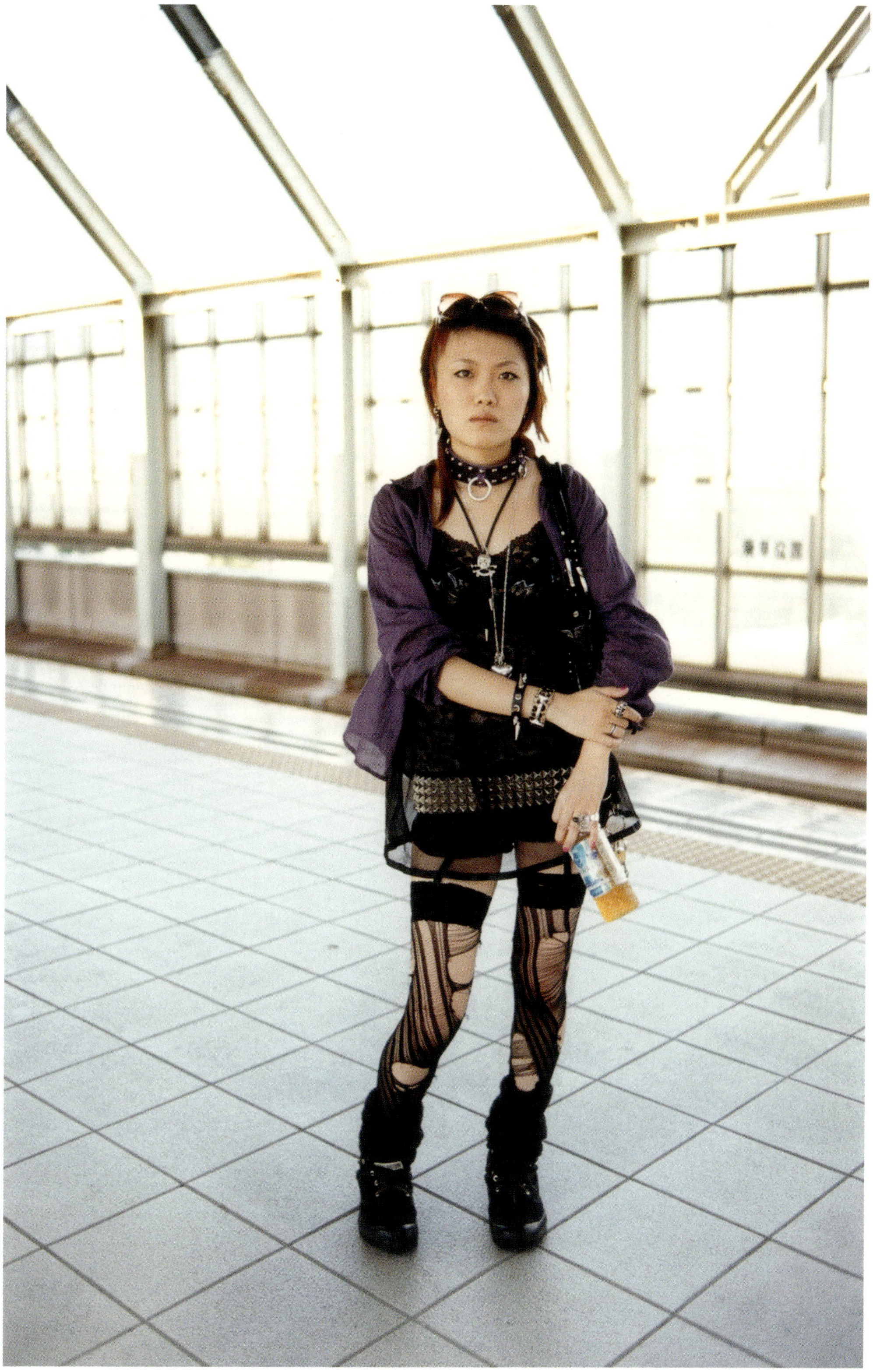

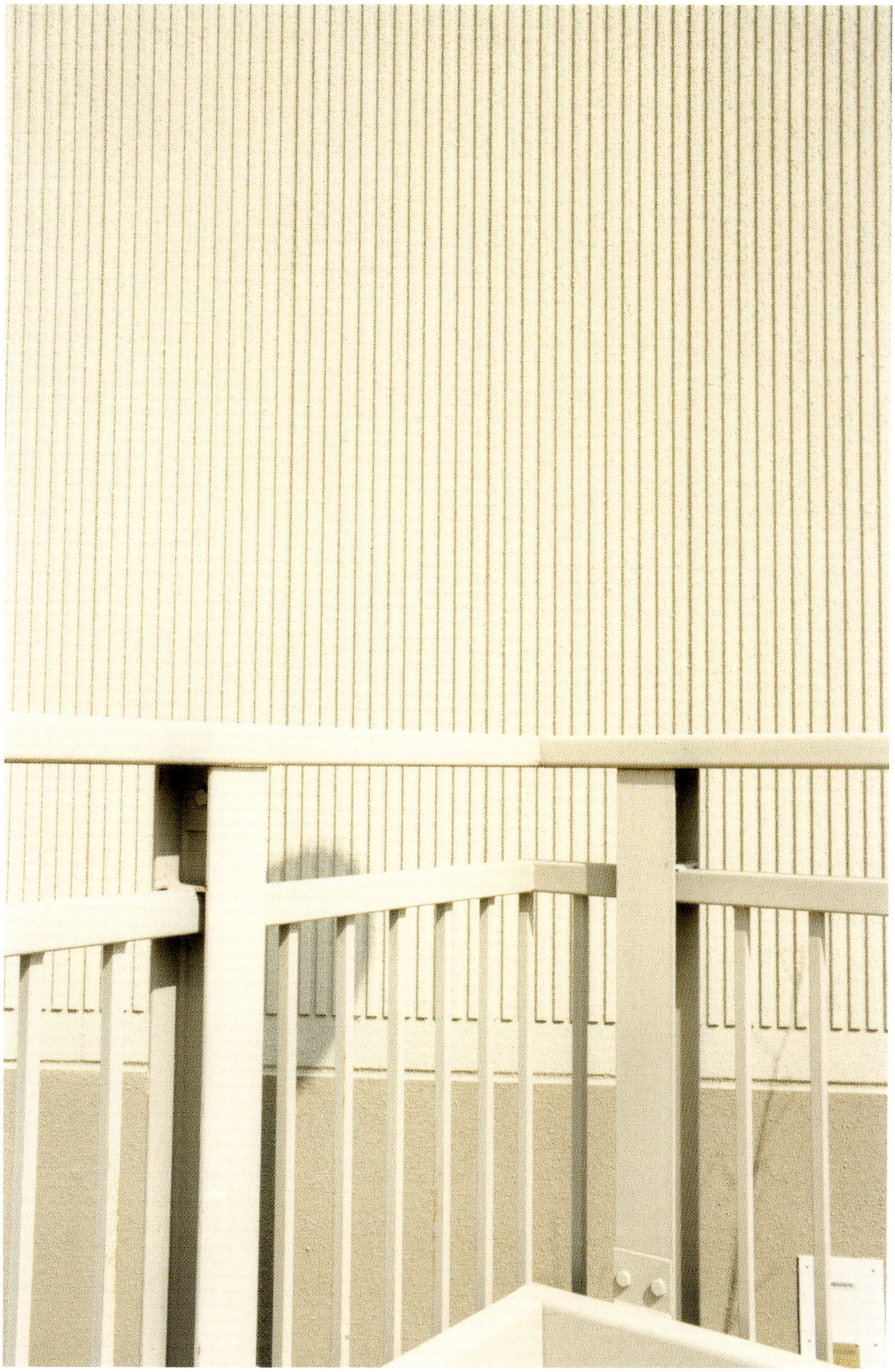

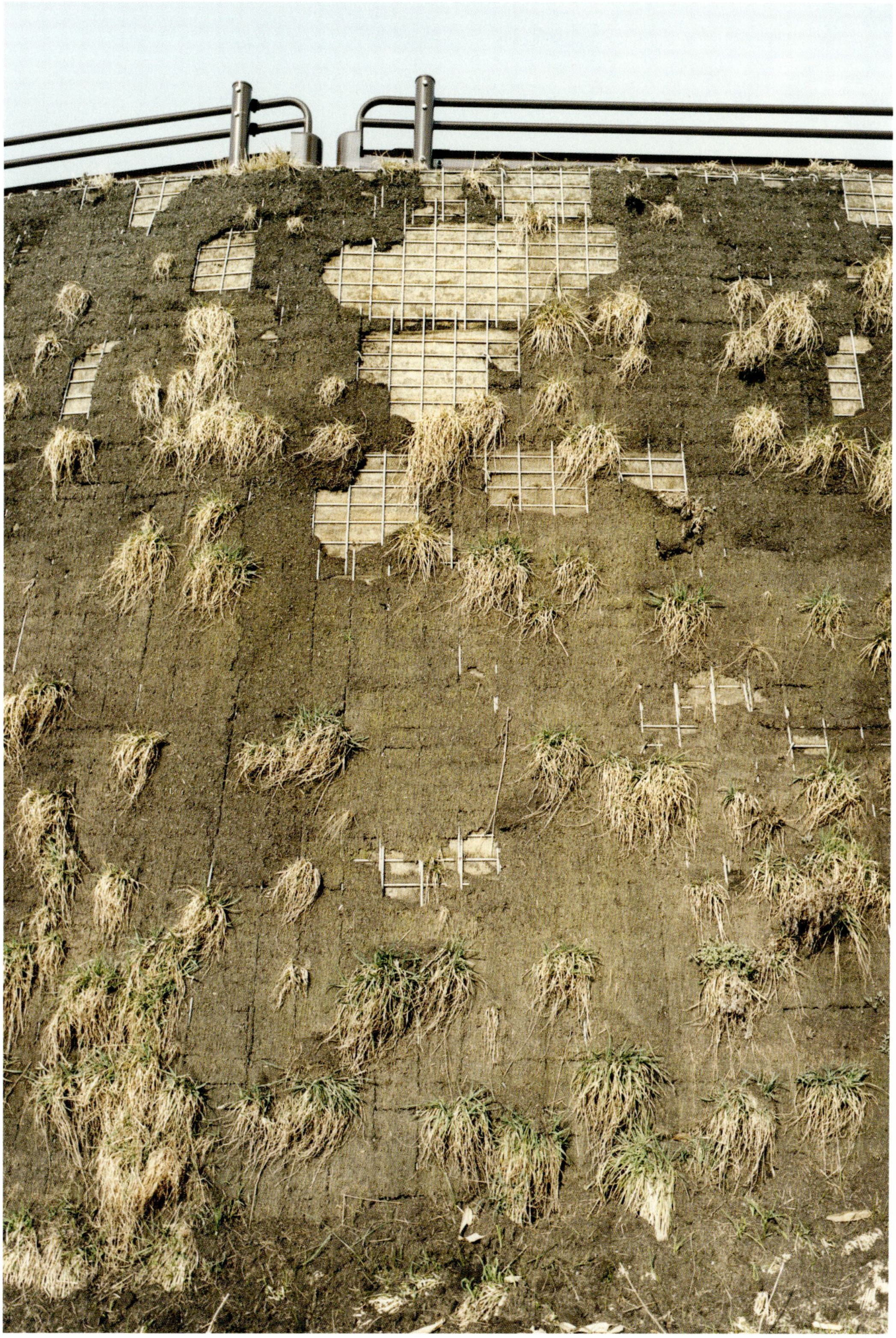

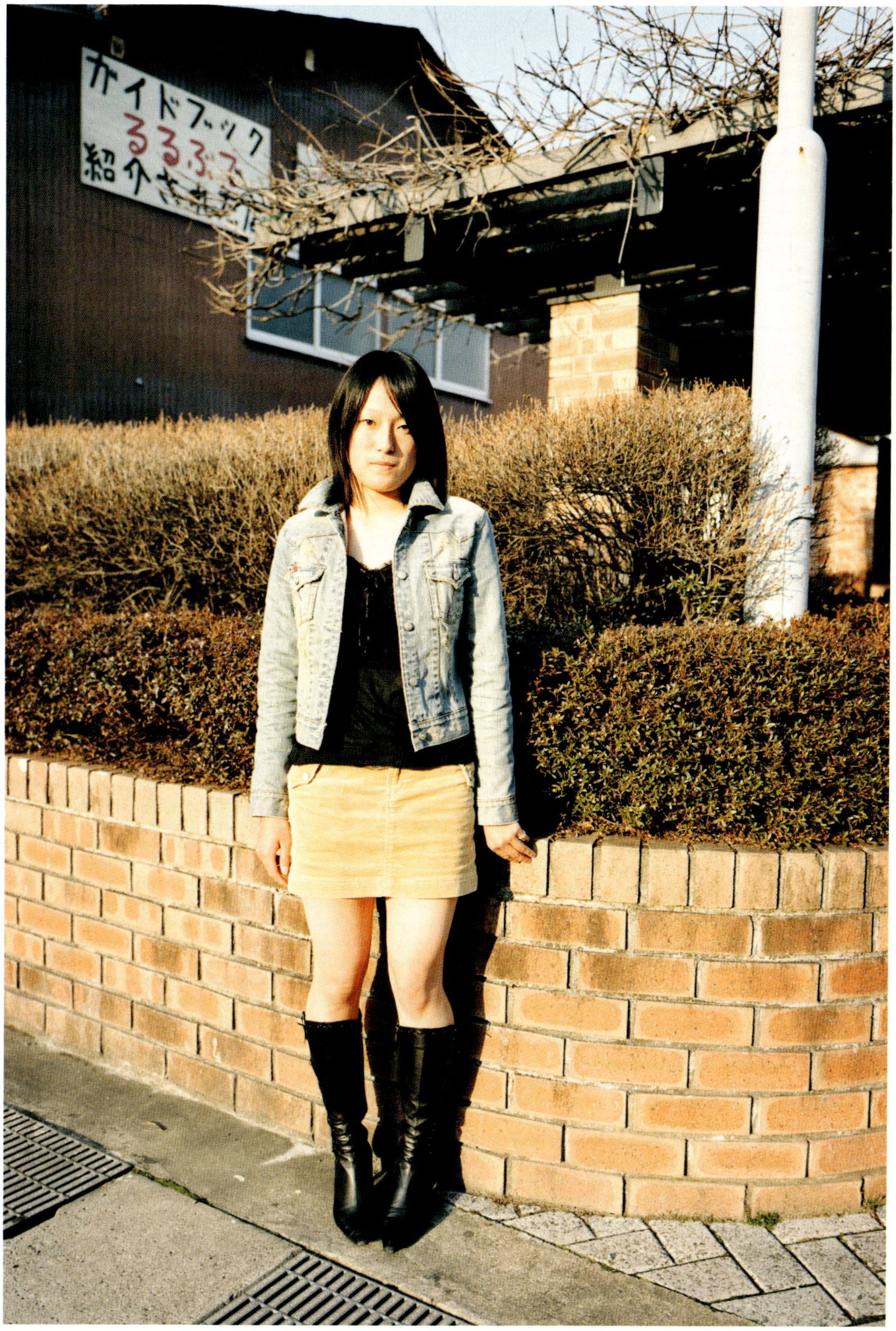
ガイドブック
るるぶ

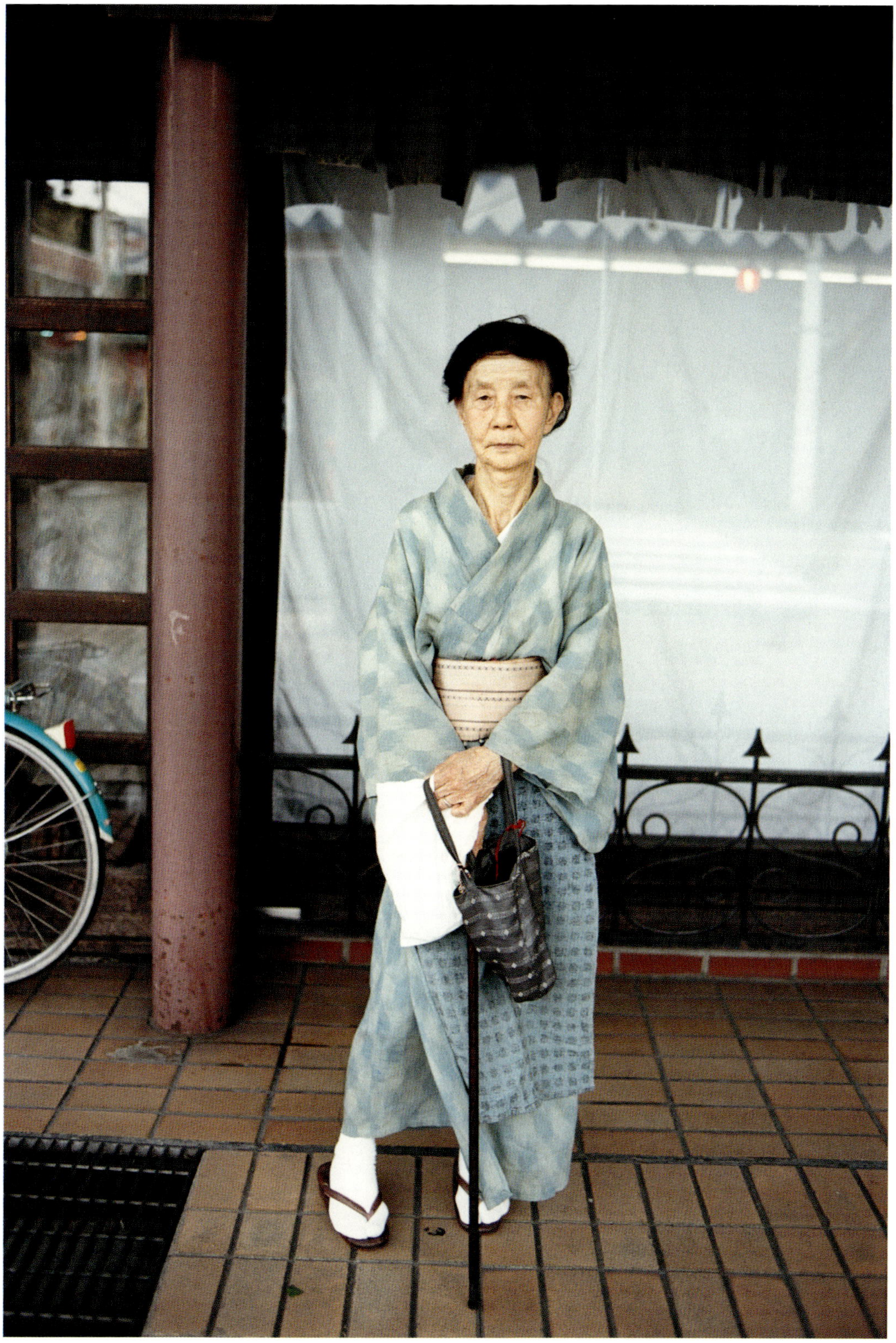

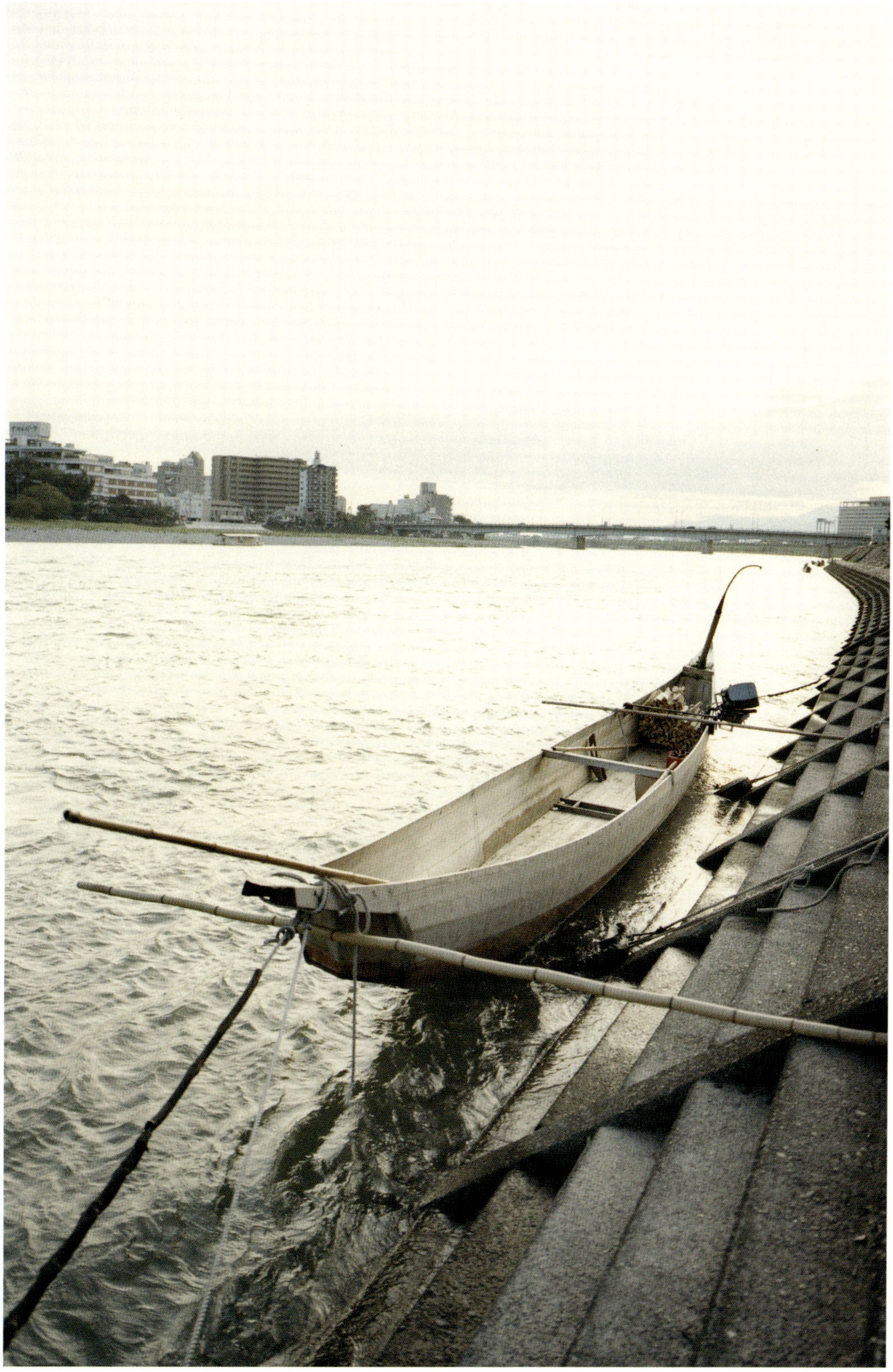

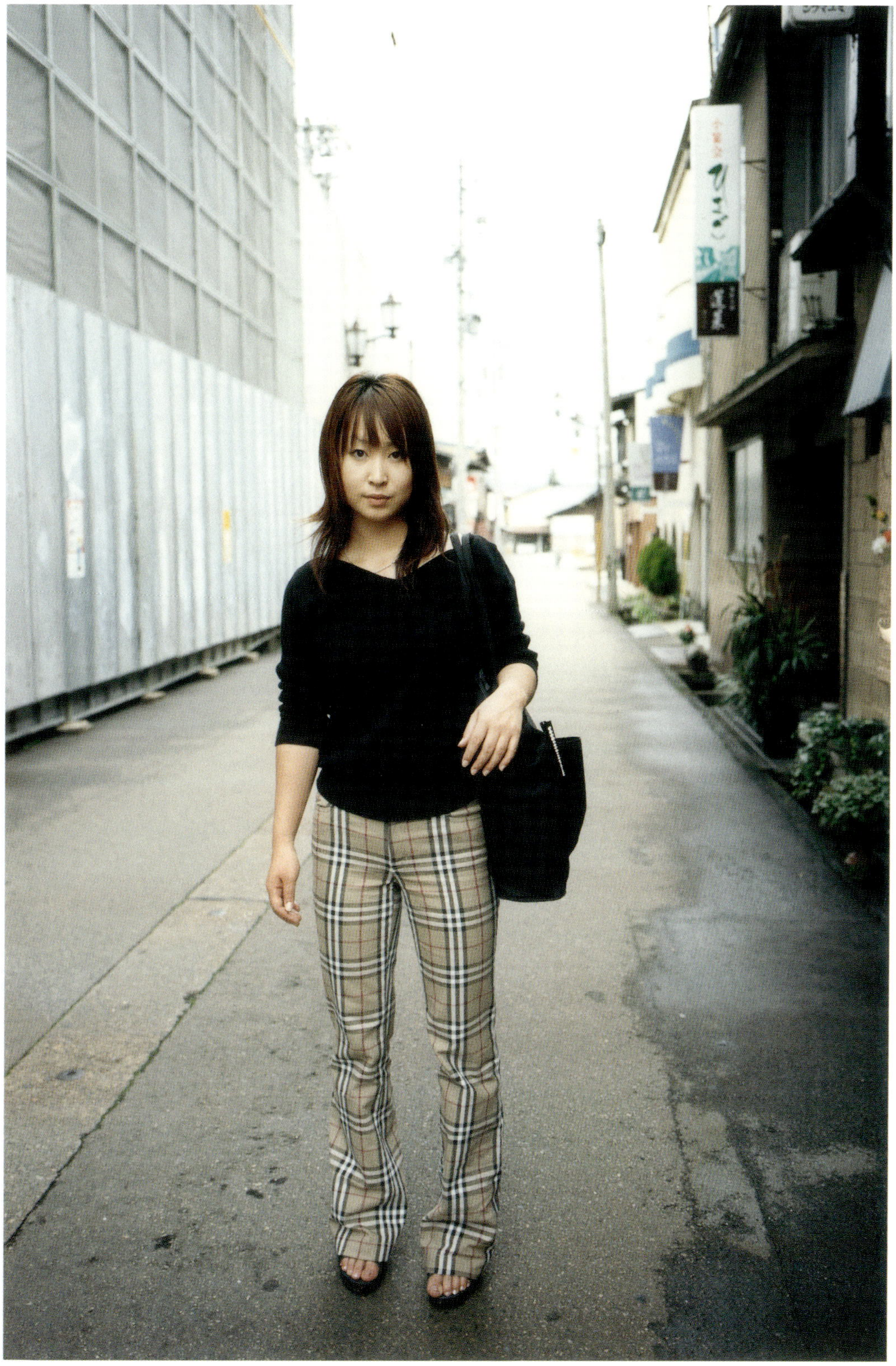

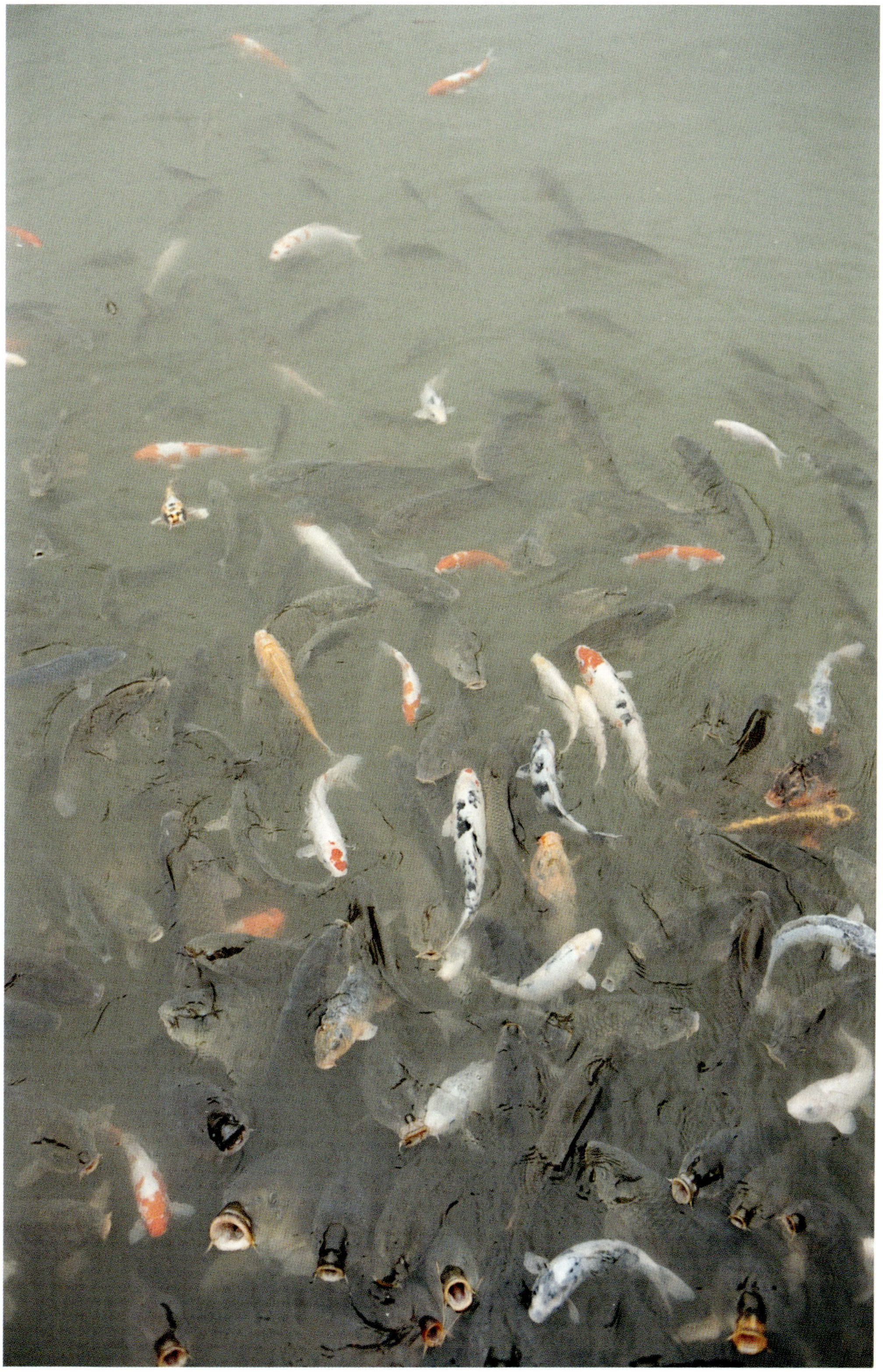

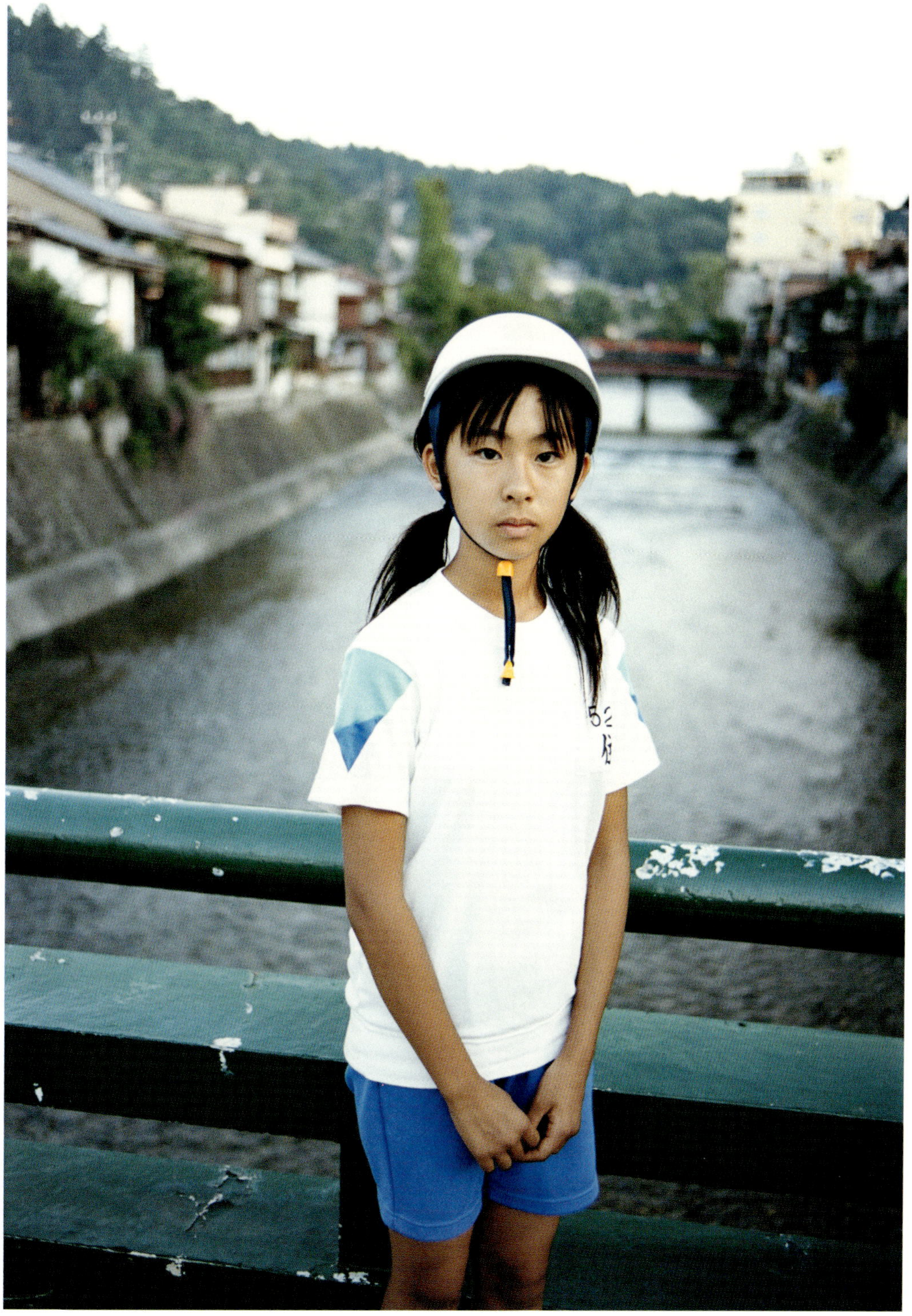

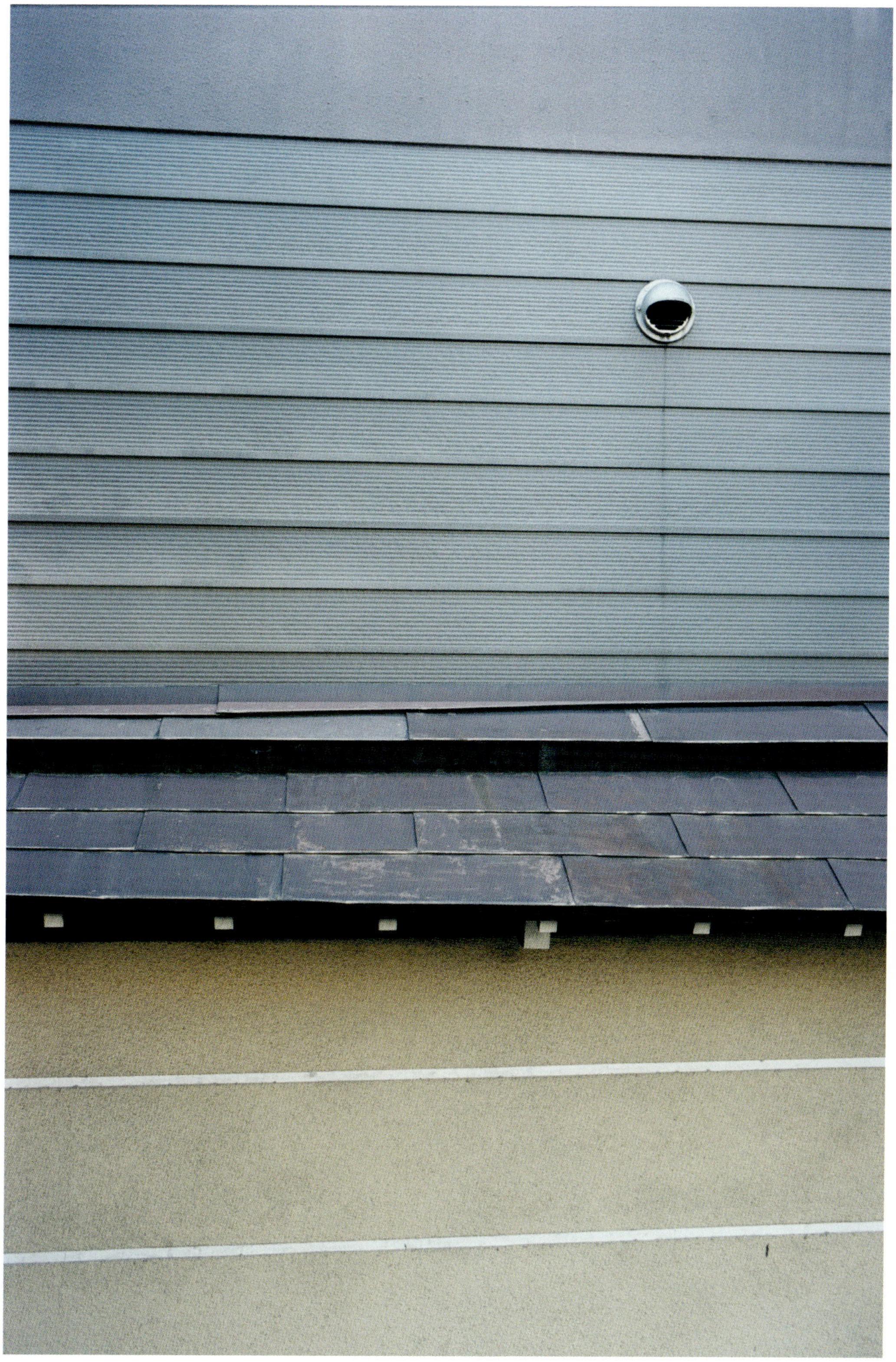

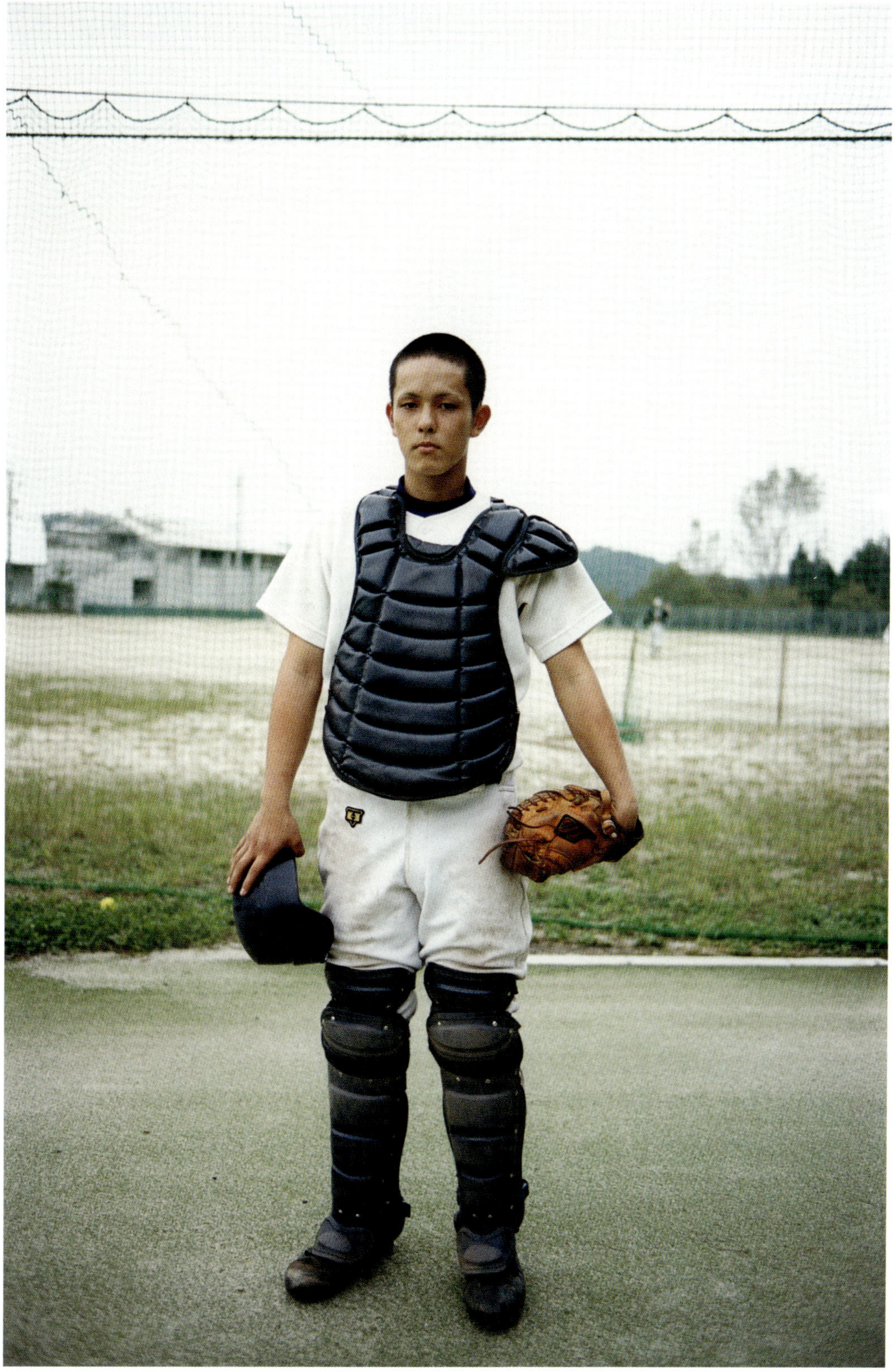

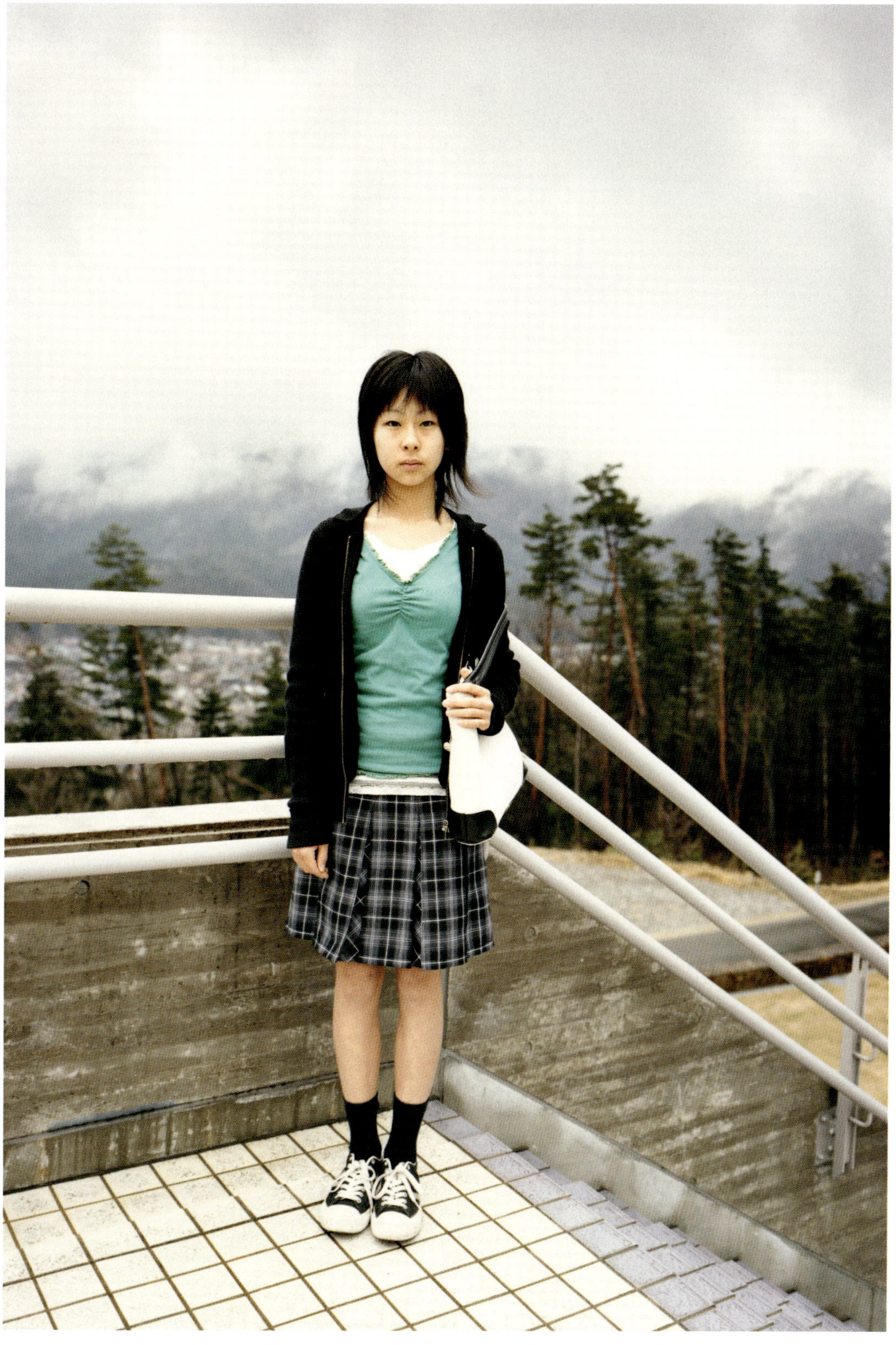

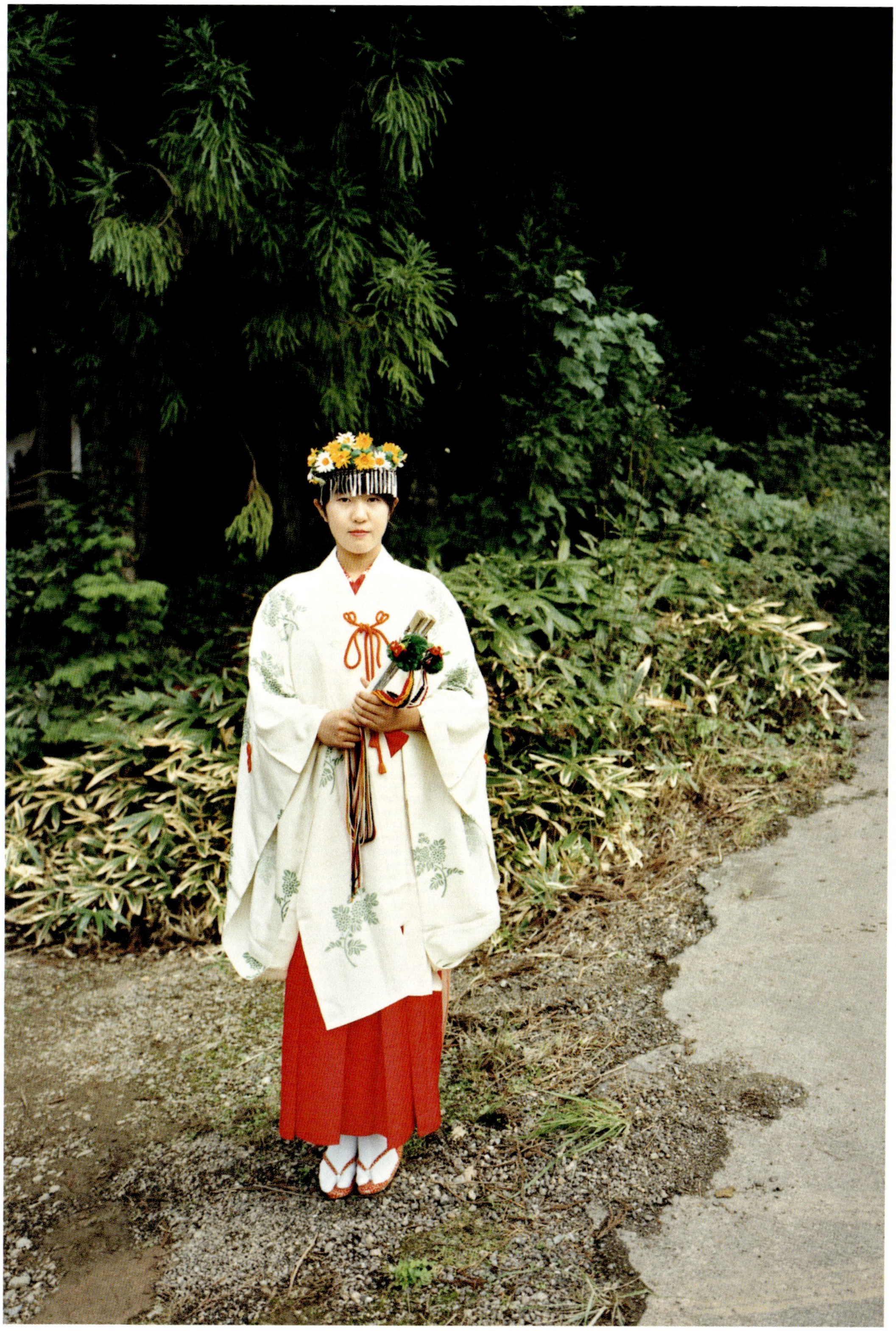

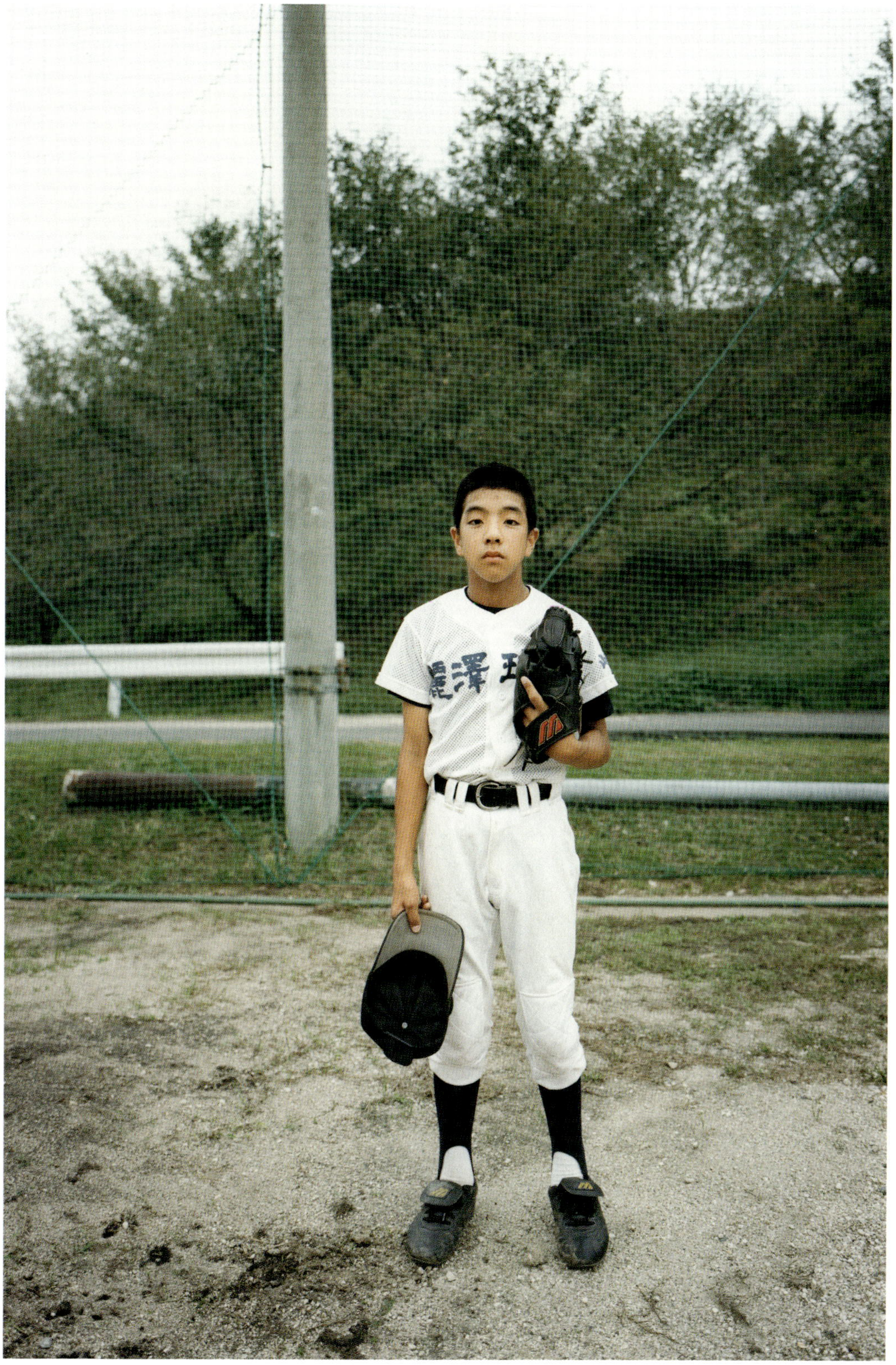

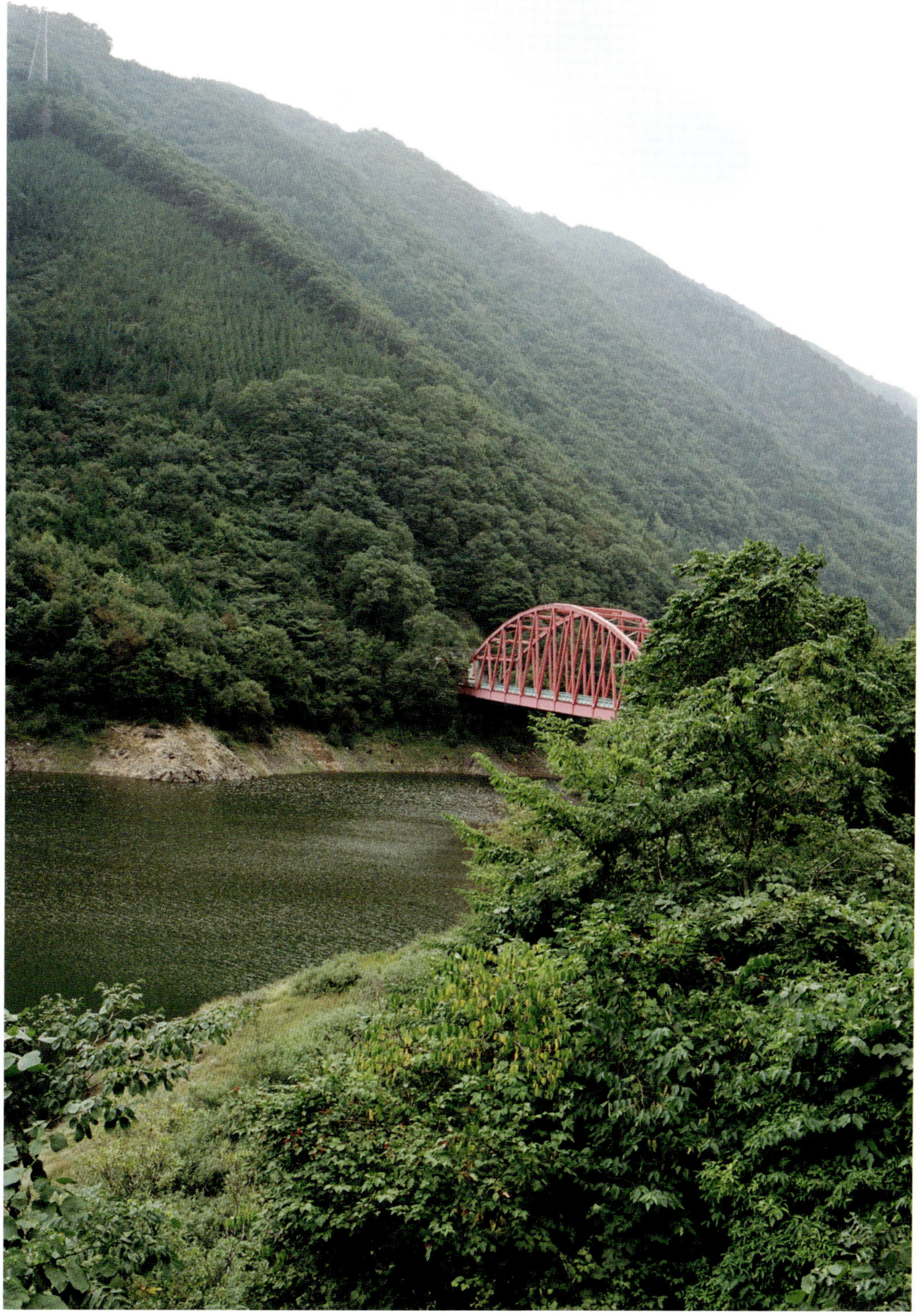

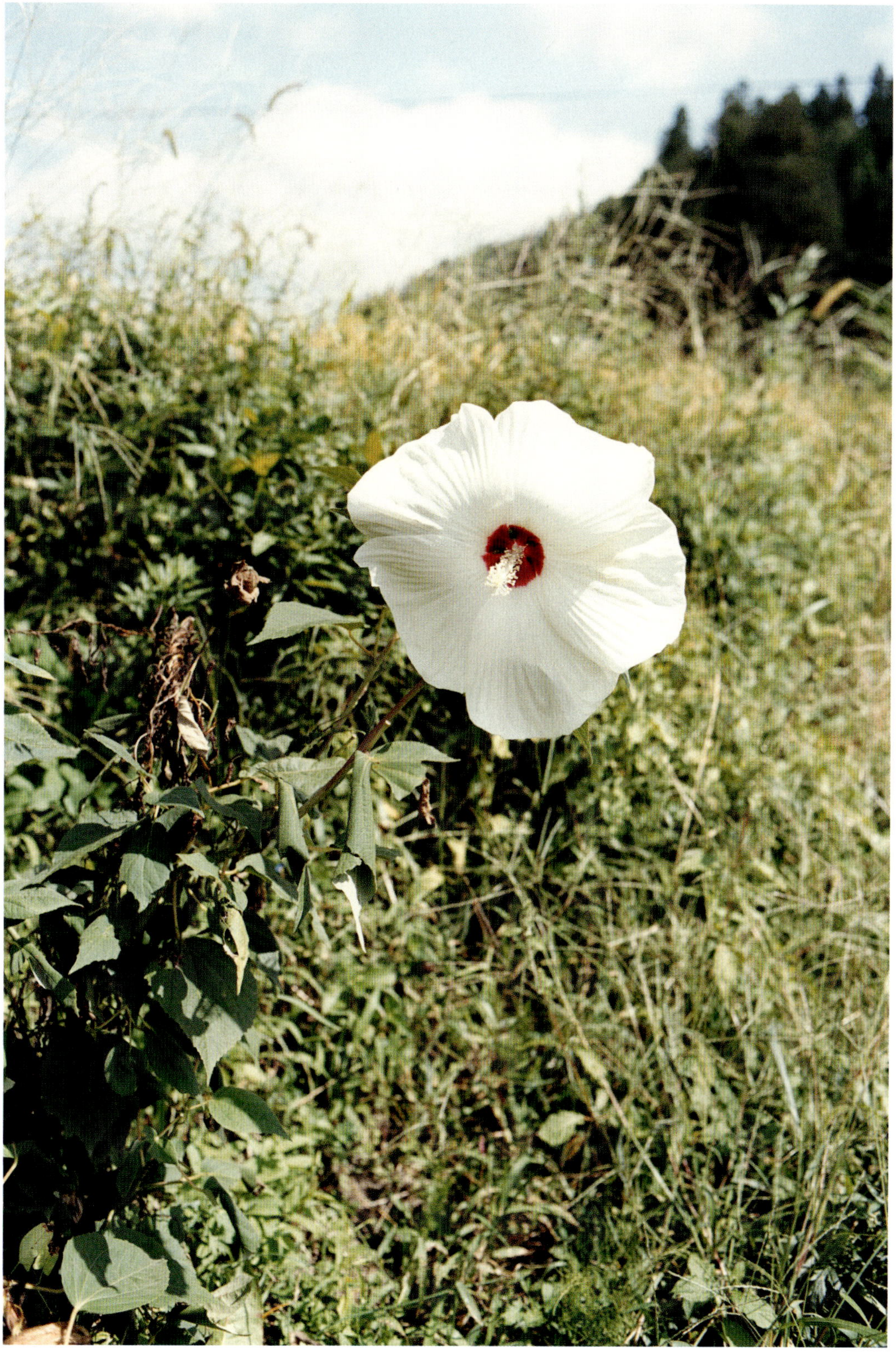

芙蓉

Watering flowers. On an experience with Japan

There are two categories of travellers to Japan: those who admire the tradition and myths, who are entranced by Japan; and those who consider Japan an alienated society and thus further advanced than all Western societies. One can see from Jitka Hanzlová's images, all of them made in Gifu Prefecture, that she is well aware of both modes of observation or both fixations. However, she belongs in neither camp. She is certainly not a sociologist with a camera.

Actually, things had pointed toward her becoming one. The school of photography in Essen was ambitious and strict, with a strong tendency towards social criticism. Hanzlová had washed up in Essen more by coincidence than design, having quit her home village of Rokytník in East Bohemia and then fled to the West from Prague, the Czechoslovak capital. There was never any doubt that the Czech student would become a photographer. However, the shape her photography took evolved from the political-historical fog of the end of the Soviet Empire: Jitka, returning to the village of Rokytník years later, gathered up the broken fragments of Socialism and discovered on the back of them enchanting miniatures of rural life somewhere between rituals and absentmindedness. Her pale portrait-format images evoked two things: a concept of the political landscape and a lively sense of portraiture. The "Rokytník" cycle of images was stunningly complete in itself and the differences to the Essen school striking. Her photographs are not just unideological; they are truly anti-ideological.

Later, when she started portraying the "inhabitants" of large cities, when she sketched masks of femininity, it emerged that she had developed the miniatures from Rokytník into a veritable style. Or people considered it a style. The matte gleam of her portraits always contained both, a sense of place and a sense of the person, visualizing a paradox, namely the determinacy of an existence in swiftly changing conditions.

When she started photography in earnest, Thomas Ruff's full-frontal portraits were already on show in museums. Ruff is exactly her contemporary and only photographed in his own studio; the lighting was carefully orchestrated, the formats truly monumental. Hanzlová's photography was the opposite on all counts. She never had the hubris to invite a model to come and sit for her. Instead, she goes out and hunts for them. It may be a coincidence that "being on the path" is a Buddhist virtue, but in this regard it seems inevitable that there would be a Japanese chapter in Hanzlová's oeuvre. In Gifu Prefecture she found the urban spaces and countryside she wanted, an alternation of small-small and high-tech, urban stages and social interiors. Just as there are politicians who walk along shaking hands with everyone at the same time, so she communicates through photography. The model understands the need for an encounter, the logic with which his or her own path crosses that of the photographer. The models are not examples of anything specific, and they notice this. Yes, you can sense the tension that arose from being chosen and providing information, having to provide information, having to state something about oneself that is in part authentic and in part only a wish, has already happened or remains to be realized. Here we can discern something that sets Jitka Hanzlová apart from almost all contemporary photographers: she has a notion of home. Just as she says her models "are rooted in the Earth" – or not – that is what she sets out to establish.

Europeans travel to very few countries in the world, perhaps only Japan and India, with the expectation that they will experience something unusual that goes far beyond what is considered "worth knowing". This turns the travellers, unlike those who have stayed at home, into bearers of secrets, or they convince themselves they are. As early as the nineteenth century, when travellers searching for an education published their record of their Grand Tour, or when a little later the earliest photographic albums you could buy showed the pyramids, travellers to Japan and India most probably tended to be writers, by profession or by dint of the occasion, as were travellers to Kenya or Argentina.

The biographic genre has blossomed since those reports by travellers of the Grand Tour. Those back home wanted to know how the traveller fared and why. This gave artists their chance, liberated from the tasks of studying the particular country. The latest novel on Japan was written by Jean-Philippe Toussaint. There, the narrator follows an impressive lady from the fashion world to Tokyo – he calls her Marie. It is a real adventure shaped by the way the lifeworld of the designer so wooed drifts apart from that of her lover, who trails behind, both of them crushed by the change of place, the alien nature of the gestures and language, the mysterious technology, a small earthquake in the very first night. Strangely, the narrator takes a small flask with him containing a liquid that destroys everything, of which he is just as afraid as of his nebulous plans of what to do with it. At the very end of the novel, which is entitled *Making Love*, he gets rid of the weapon, in a museum garden behind the building itself:

"Close to me, on the ground and in the shade, stood a tiny, single, very small flower. I contemplated it, the light of the moon illuminated it softly and created pale tender reflections on its white and mauve petals. I didn't know what sort of a flower it was, one that grew in the wild, a violet, a pansy, and without taking another step, tired, broken, and exhausted, in order to bring things to a final close I emptied the bottle of hydrochloric acid over the flower, which immediately turned into a cloud of steam and a terrible stench, contracting, curling up, shrinking into itself. Nothing remained other than a crater that steamed in the pallid light of the moon, and the feeling that I had triggered this infinitely small catastrophe."

While the traveller to India seeks to forget himself, immersed in a different era, the traveller to Japan is thrown into a condensed version of the present. The country's cultural complexity shoots through the visitor like an electric current. The eye of a detective is needed to grasp all the everyday things. No one in this country needs the visitor (no one begs, no one speaks to him). However mysterious the social rules and mores may be, they are just that, can be deciphered, by analogies and differences. One can be overwhelmed by the wish to dissolve in this order; it is not an order of beautiful things, but a beautiful order of common things.

Jitka Hanzlová deciphers them by not giving in to the temptation to render the strange and foreign as enigmatic. If one considers Werner Bischof's *Japan*, which he made fifty years ago, and compares it to Hanzlová's current book, then one observes the paradigm shift. Back then, Bischof was on an Asian version of the Grand Tour, was under the spell of the task of understanding "Japan" for us or at least perhaps illustrating it. By contrast, Hanzlová simply sees with her own eyes, and she also does not need the complete realm of symbols; all she needs are bends in the road and the riverbanks in Gifu. At a pond, its depths dulled by traces of clay, she creates the exciting image of the exotically patterned fish, some of them with mouths gaping open like the ends of rubber tubes. Three black cows stand on a meadow deep in soft grass like gods we have failed to recognize. Black, web-footed birds with white faces stand in a cement garden, simply staring, the priests to such gods.

In the countryside she discerns the spirit of its inhabitants and in passers-by the reified form of the lifeworld. This is why her equivalencies are so successful, the combinations of portrait and countryside that together are more than the sum of their parts. Although she always maintains a certain distance, each image has a specific density – the way you can pack a flat-bed in such a way as to fill it and make certain nothing can move around. Even if, on closer inspection, traits of more detailed design are in evidence, a sense of the lifeworld prevails that is more physical than visual. These images have something to do with breath, which is why they also do not call for admiration; it is easy, only shortly after closing the book, to start thinking they were something you experienced yourself.

Jitka Hanzlová's portraits are fully frontal and casual, have become very influential ever since *Rokytník* came out, but the work is unparalleled, or put differently, her images precisely cannot be placed in the lineage of August Sander. Hanzlová does not want to prove anything; she wants us to experience something. Her prior knowledge is not a concept and her interpretation is not intended to show us something. She may be a female West European photographer, but not a typical one; she will forever remain a refugee from Socialism, even if it is now history. All those who saved their skins facing those risks know something about human individuality that otherwise possibly remains concealed.

According to Sigmund Freud, the human soul is made up of three agencies, the Id (the unconscious and the instincts), the Ego (the task of Freudian therapy was to strengthen it) and the Super-Ego, the tentacles of conscience. The West's fascination with the Asian collective led to the individual being under-estimated; in the late 1930s even that great architect Bruno Taut guilelessly considered the Japanese "ants". As regards travellers to Japan and their passions, one could say that the traditionalists have fallen prey to the Japanese Super-Ego, the post-modernists to the Japanese Id. The former love the raked pebble gardens, the latter the neon hustle of the backstreet bars. It may to this day be true that in Japan the Id and the Super-Ego are strong, antagonists in a way that remains inexplicable from a Viennese point of view. It is even harder to identify the Japanese Ego, which truly seems to be masked, and even if it is accorded less space (which can happen in Japan) this does not mean that it is second in complexity to the European or American Ego. The opposite is probably the case. Jitka Hanzlová, a nomad of encounters, intuited this. But she can't prove it; that is her strength.

Ulf Erdmann Ziegler
March 2003

Blumen gießen. Über eine Erfahrung mit Japan

Japanfahrer fallen in zwei Lager: die einen bewundern Tradition und Mythos, sie sind von Japan verzaubert; die anderen betrachten Japan als entfremdete Gesellschaft, und als solche weiter fortgeschritten als jede westliche. Man sieht Jitka Hanzlovás Bildern, entstanden in der Präfektur Gifu, an, dass ihr die beiden Modi der Betrachtung – oder Fixierung – geläufig sind, aber sie gehört weder zum einen Lager noch zum anderen. Überhaupt ist sie nicht die Soziologin mit der Kamera.

Eigentlich hätte sie eine werden sollen. Die Essener Schule der Fotografie war eine ehrgeizige und strenge, mit einem starken Hang zur Gesellschaftskritik. Hanzlová war eher zufällig nach Essen geschwemmt worden, weggegangen aus ihrem ostböhmischen Dorf Rokytník, geflüchtet aus Prag, Hauptstadt der Tschecheslowakei, in den Westen. Dass die tschechische Schülerin Fotografin geworden wäre, steht außer Zweifel. Die Gestalt ihrer Fotografie jedoch wuchs aus dem politisch-historischen Nebel am Ende des sowjetischen Imperiums: Jitka, nach Jahren zurückgekehrt in das Dorf Rokytník, sammelte die Scherben des Sozialismus auf und entdeckte auf deren Rückseiten bezaubernde Miniaturen ländlichen Lebens zwischen Ritualen und Selbstvergessenheit. Ihre blassen Hochformate evozierten zweierlei: einen Begriff von politischer Landschaft und eine lebendige Portraitistik. Die Vollständigkeit des Bilderzyklus „Rokytník" war umwerfend; die Differenz zur Essener Schule offenkundig. Ihre Fotografie ist nicht nur un-, sondern geradezu antiideologisch.

Später, als sie die „Bewohner" großer Städte portraitierte, als sie Masken der Weiblichkeit skizzierte, zeigte sich, dass sie die Miniaturen von Rokytník ausgearbeitet hatte zu einem Stil. Oder man hielt das für einen Stil. Der matte Glanz ihrer Portraits barg immer beides, Ortssinn und Menschensinn, so dass ein Paradox sichtbar wurde, nämlich die Bestimmtheit einer Existenz in rasch sich wandelnden Verhältnissen.

Als sie ernsthaft zu fotografieren begann, waren die frontalen Porträts von Thomas Ruff – gleicher Jahrgang – bereits im Museum angekommen. Ruff fotografierte nur im eigenen Atelier; die Lichtsetzung war konfektioniert; die Formate monumental. Hanzlovás Fotografie ist also in jedem Punkt das Gegenteil. Niemals hätte sie die Hybris, ein Modell einzubestellen. Sie geht hinaus und findet es. Es ist Zufall, dass „auf dem Weg zu sein" eine buddhistische Tugend ist, aber insofern schien ein japanisches Kapitel in Hanzlovás Werk unvermeidbar. In der Präfektur Gifu fand sie ihren Stadt-

und Landschaftsraum, ein Wechsel von Klein-klein und High-tech, urbaner Bühne und sozialem Interieur. So wie manche Politiker sich fortbewegen und dabei jedem die Hand geben, betreibt die Fotografin Kommunikation. Das Modell begreift die Notwendigkeit der Begegnung, die Logik, mit der sich der eigene Weg und der der Fotografin kreuzen. Die Modelle sind keine Beispiele für irgendetwas, und das merken sie. Ja, man spürt sehr wohl die Spannung, die darin liegt, gewählt zu sein und Auskunft zu geben, geben zu müssen; von sich selbst etwas zu behaupten, was teils authentisch ist und teils nur herbeigewünscht, bereits eingetreten oder noch zu verwirklichen. Hier zeigt sich etwas, was Jitka Hanzlová von fast allen zeitgenössischen Fotografen unterscheidet: Dass sie einen Begriff von Heimat hat. Wie ihre Modelle „mit der Erde verwurzelt sind" (J.H.) – oder nicht –, das will sie wissen.

Nur wenige Länder der Welt – vielleicht nur Japan und Indien – werden von Europäern bereist mit der Erwartung, etwas Ungewöhnliches in Erfahrung zu bringen, das weit über „Wissenwertes" hinausgeht. Das macht die Reisenden, im Vergleich zu den Daheimgebliebenen, zu Geheimnisträgern, oder das bilden sie sich ein. So wie früh im 19. Jahrhundert der Bildungsreisende über seine Grand Tour einen Bericht veröffentlichte, oder wenig später die frühesten käuflichen fotografischen Alben Pyramiden zeigten, sind Japan- und Indienreisende mit größerer Wahrscheinlichkeit auch Publizisten, per Beruf oder Gelegenheit, als Reisende nach Kenia oder Argentinien.

Dabei blüht, seit den Berichten der Reisenden der „Grand Tour", das biographische Genre. Man möchte daheim schon wissen, wie es dem Reisenden ergangen ist und warum. So kommen Künstler zu ihrem Recht, die von den Aufgaben der Landeskunde freigestellt sind. Der jüngste Japanroman stammt von Jean-Philippe Toussaint. Da folgt der Erzähler einer imposanten Lady der Modewelt nach Tokio – er nennt sie Marie –, eine abenteuerliche Reise, die bestimmt ist durch die auseinanderstrebende Lebenswelt der umworbenen Gestalterin und ihrem abgehängten Liebhaber, beide aufgerieben durch den Ortswechsel und die Fremdheit der Gesten und der Sprache, die geheimnisvolle Technik, ein kleines Erdbeben in der ersten Nacht. Merkwürdigerweise trägt der Erzähler ein Fläschchen mit einer alles vernichtenden Flüssigkeit bei sich, vor der er sich mindestens ebenso fürchtet wie vor seinen diffusen Plänen, was damit zu tun sei. Ganz am Ende des Romans, der „Sich lieben" heißt, entledigt er sich im Museumsgarten, jenseits eines Museums, der Waffe:

„Auf dem Boden nahe bei mir stand, im Schatten, winzig, eine einzelne ganz kleine Blume. Ich betrachtete sie, das Licht des Mondes beleuchtete sie sanft und ließ auf ihren weißen und malvenfarbenen Blütenblättern fahle zarte Reflexe erstrahlen. Ich wußte nicht, was für eine Blume es war, eine wildwachsende Blume, ein Veilchen, ein Stiefmütterchen, und ohne einen Schritt weiter zu tun, müde, gebrochen, erschöpft, leerte ich, um endlich Schluß zu machen, die Flasche Salzsäure über der Blume aus, die sich mit einem Schlag in einer Wolke aus Dampf und fürchterlichem Gestank zusammenzog, in sich kräuselte, zusammenschrumpfte. Nichts blieb übrig außer einem Krater, der im matten Licht des Mondscheins dampfte, und dem Gefühl, diese unendlich kleine Katastrophe ausgelöst zu haben."

Während der Indienfahrer sich selbst zu vergessen sucht, eintaucht in eine andere Zeit, ist der Japanfahrer in eine kondensierte Gegenwart geworfen. Die kulturelle Komplexität des Landes fährt in den Besucher wie elektrischer Strom. Detektivische Aufmerksamkeit ist vonnöten, um Dinge des Alltags zu erfassen. Niemand in diesem Land braucht den Besucher (niemand bettelt, niemand spricht ihn an). So geheimnisvoll das Regelwerk des Sozialen sein mag, es ist eines, es lässt sich entschlüsseln, durch Analogien und Differenzen. Es überfällt einen der Wunsch, aufzugehen in dieser Ordnung; nicht eine Ordnung von schönen Dingen, sondern eine schöne Ordnung gewöhnlicher Dinge.

Diese enträtselt Jitka Hanzlová, indem sie der Versuchung, das Fremde zu verrätseln, nicht nachgibt. Betrachtet man Werner Bischofs „Japan" – entstanden vor fünfzig Jahren – und Jitka Hanzlovás gegenwärtiges Buch im Vergleich, kann man einen Paradigmenwechsel beobachten. Bischof war noch auf asiatischer Grand Tour, er steht unter dem Bann des Auftrags, Japan „für uns" zu verstehen oder vielleicht auch nur zu illustrieren; während Hanzlová nur mit den eigenen Augen sieht, und sie braucht auch nicht das komplette Reich der Zeichen, es reichen die Straßenbiegungen und Flußufer von Gifu. An einem von Lehmspuren blinden Teich entsteht das aufregende Bild exotisch gemusterter Fische, einige Mäuler offen wie Gummischläuche. Drei schwarze Kühe haben sich auf einer watteweichen Wiese aufgestellt wie verkannte Götter. Schwarze Pechvögel im Zementgarten, herrisch glotzend, geben die Priester dazu.

Sie erkennt in der Landschaft den Geist der Bewohner und in den Passanten die Verdinglichung ihrer Lebenswelt. Deshalb glücken ihr auch die Pendants, Kombinationen von Porträt und Landschaft, die gemeinsam mehr sind als die

Summe ihrer Teile. Obwohl sie einen gewissen Abstand wählt, hat jedes Bild seine spezifische Dichte, so wie man eine Ladefläche bepacken kann, dass sie voll ist und nichts rutscht. Auch wenn man, genau besehen, Züge detaillierter Gestaltung erkennen kann, dominiert eine Auffassung der Lebenswelt, die eher leiblich als visuell ist. Diese Bilder haben etwas mit dem Atem zu tun, weshalb sie auch nicht nach Bewunderung rufen; leicht hält man sie, kaum ist das Buch geschlossen, für einen Teil der eigenen Erfahrung.

Jitka Hanzlovás Porträts, frontal und beiläufig, sind seit dem Erscheinen von „Rokytník" sehr einflussreich gewesen, aber sie ist unerreicht, oder anders gesagt, fallen ihre Werke eben nicht in die Tradition August Sanders. Hanzlová will nichts belegen, sie will etwas in Erfahrung bringen. Ihr Vorwissen ist nicht Konzept und ihre Deutung kein Zeigen. Sie ist zwar eine westeuropäische Fotografin, aber nicht die aus dem Bilderbuch; sie bleibt für immer Flüchtling aus dem Sozialismus, auch wenn dieser Geschichte ist. Wer mit diesem Risiko sein Fell gerettet hat, weiß etwas von der Individualität des Menschen, das anderen möglicherweise verborgen bleibt.

Nach Sigmund Freud besteht die menschliche Seele aus drei Instanzen, dem Es (Unbewusstes und Trieb), dem Ich (dieses zu stärken wurde Aufgabe der Freudschen Therapie) und dem Über-Ich, das Gewissen als Krake. Die Faszination des Westens mit dem asiatischen Kollektiv hat dazu geführt, dass das Individuum unterschätzt wurde; selbst der große Architekt Bruno Taut bezeichnet die Japaner, am Ende der 1930er Jahre, arglos als „Ameisen". Was nun die Japanfahrer und ihre Passionen betrifft, könnte man sagen, dass die Traditionalisten dem japanischen Über-Ich verfallen sind, die Postmodernen dem Japanischen Es. Die einen lieben die geharkten Gärten, die anderen das Remmidemmi der Hinterstuben. Selbst bis heute mag gelten, dass das Es und das Über-Ich in Japan stark sind, Antagonisten in einer Weise, die von Wien aus unbegreiflich bleibt. Schwerer auszumachen, geradezu maskiert mag das japanische Ich sein, und selbst wenn sein Platz knapper wäre (das kann in Japan schon vorkommen), heißt das nicht, dass es an Komplexität dem europäischen oder amerikanischen nachstehe. Das Gegenteil ist wahrscheinlich. Jitka Hanzlová, als Nomadin der Begegnung, hat das geahnt. Beweisen kann sie's nicht; das ist ihre Stärke.

Ulf Erdmann Ziegler
im März 2003

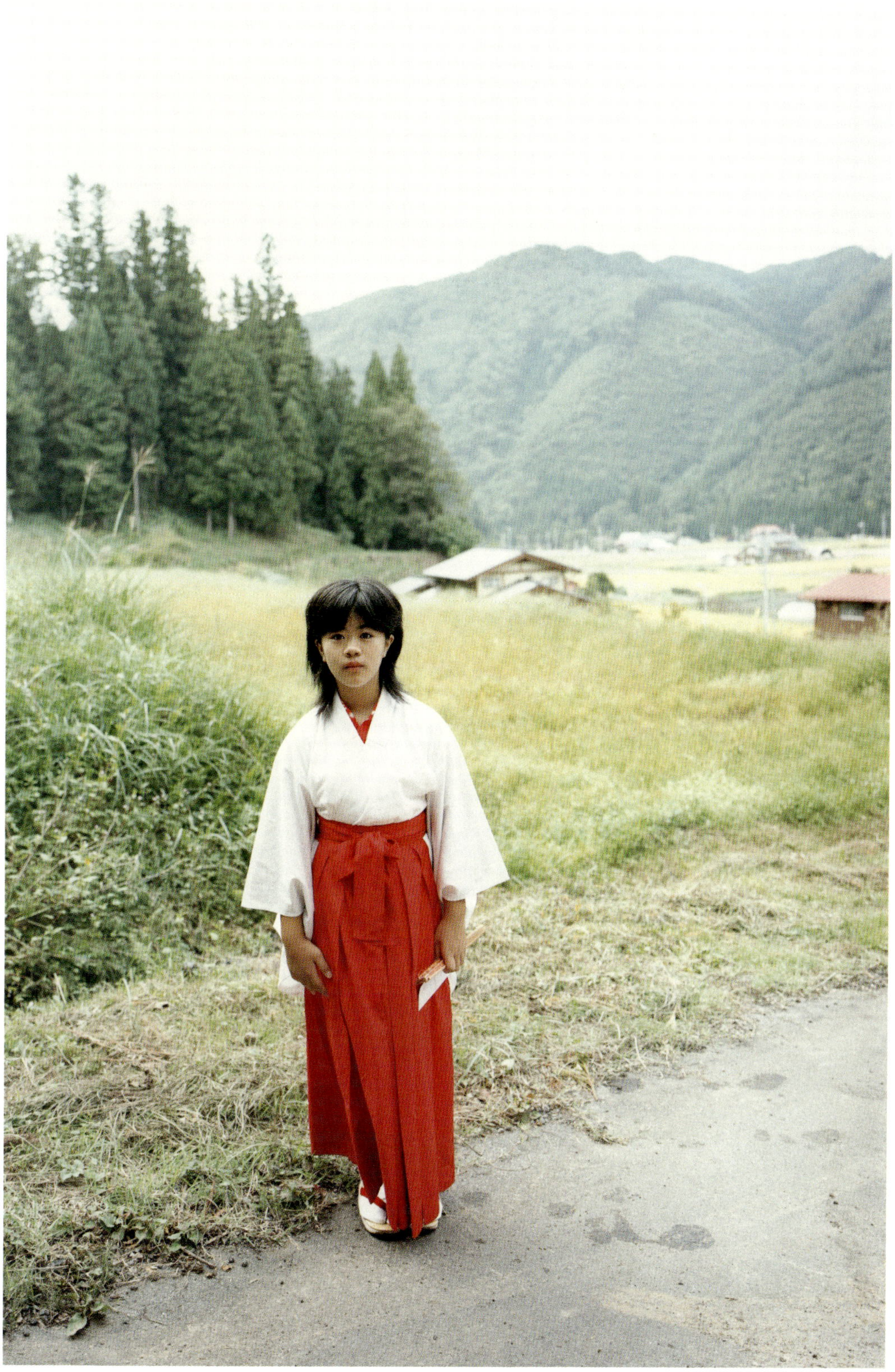

Dieses Projekt ist in der japanischen Präfektur Gifu, in den Jahren 2004 und 2006 in Zusammenarbeit mit European Eyes On Japan / Japan Today entstanden, mit Unterstützung des EU-Japan Committees.
Mein Dank gilt allen, die an diesem Projekt beteiligt waren, insbesondere dem Japan Fest Committee mit Shuji Kogi, Mikiko Kikuta, Noriko Kodera, Mr. Kodera, Yuki Minamimoto und allen Portraitierten für ihre Bereitschaft, Humor und Offenheit meine Idee in Japan zu realisieren. Sylvia Pöhlmann, Axel Stoffers für ihre Unterstützung, Ulf Erdmann Ziegler für den finalen Text und Jana für ihr geduldiges Warten während meiner Abwesenheit.

This project in Gifu Prefecture in Japan evolved in 2004 and 2006 in cooperation with European Eyes On Japan / Japan Today and with the support of the EU-Japan Committee.
My thanks go to everyone who was involved in this project, especially the Japan Fest Committee with Shuji Kogi, Mikiko Kikuta, Noriko Kodera, Mr. Kodera, Yuki Minamimoto and to all the persons portrayed for their willingness, humour and openness toward realizing my idea in Japan. Sylvia Pöhlmann and Axel Stoffers for their support, Ulf Erdmann Ziegler for the final text and Jana for waiting patiently while I was away.

COTTON ROSE

Published in 2017 in an edition of 1000 books

Book design: Jitka Hanzlová
Typography: Sylvia Pöhlmann
Translation: Jeremy Gaines
Scans and colour separations by Steidl
Production: Duncan Whyte and Gerhard Steidl
Printing: Steidl, Göttingen

Steidl
Düstere Str. 4 / 37073 Göttingen, Germany
Phone +49 551 49 60 60 / Fax +49 551 49 60 649
mail@steidl.de
steidl.de

ISBN 978-3-95829-127-3
Printed in Germany by Steidl